GROWING UP AT DAD'S TABLE

Also by Lawrence Weill

Out in Front

Incarnate

I'm in the Room

The Path of Rainwater

Silas LaMontaie

Growing Up at Dad's Table

To Mateo, please enjoy and please cook for your Mom!

[signature] Weill

12/11/22

Stories and Recipes from Growing Up
in the 60's and 70's with a Single Father

by

LAWRENCE WEILL

Ⱥ
BOOKS

Adelaide Books
New York / Lisbon
2022

GROWING UP AT DAD'S TABLE

Stories and Recipes from Growing Up in the 60's and 70's
with a Single Father

By Lawrence Weill

Copyright © by Lawrence Weill

Cover design © 2022 Adelaide Books

Published by Adelaide Books, New York / Lisbon
adelaidebooks.org

Editor-in-Chief
Stevan V. Nikolic

For any information, please address Adelaide Books
at info@adelaidebooks.org

or write to:

Adelaide Books
244 Fifth Ave. Suite D27
New York, NY, 10001

ISBN: 978-1-958419-24-3
Printed in the United States of America

For All My Brothers and Sisters

Lawrence Weill

Contents

Lawrence Weill

Foreword

In the 1960's and '70's, being raised by a single father was a bit of a rarity. That my father raised three sons and two daughters by himself is a feat I find remarkable. What follows are my recollections of what that was like. We grew up primarily in the small city of Owensboro, Kentucky, where I made lifelong friends, learned about people, sometimes cheated death, and always enjoyed life. Lots of other people are included in these memories. In general, I have not given their last names, but you know who you are. The recipes included at the end of each chapter are my take on Dad's recipes, and he was a very fine cook, but, like most great home cooks, he very rarely used a recipe, so my quantities are strictly guidelines. As with all recipes, use your own taste as the best guide.

Lawrence Weill

Scuffletown

I turned six and started school in a little community known as Scuffletown. Scuffletown is still there, a smattering of houses and farms spread along the south bank of the Rapidan River in the Shenandoah Valley of Virginia. When I was a child, there was one small general store, Bowman's, which sold no perishables, but did have some basic canned goods as well as gasoline and kerosene. Few of the roads in the area were named, much less paved. To get to our house, you turned by Mr. Colvin's house. That was the only landmark there I knew. We lived in a falling down shack of a house on 138 acres of some of the most beautiful land anywhere. The house was very rugged – no phone, no electricity, no central heat, no insulation in the walls, not even running water. In fact, we carried water in gallon galvanized steel pails to fill the washtub for cooking and for baths. I was little, but I still carried a little in each pail, being sure to even out the weight before the trek up the hill. It was a long path from the well-spring, so bathwater was usually shared, baths taken consecutively. The next to the youngest of five kids, I was usually last (the baby going first of course). In summer, Dad would take us three boys to the old gravel pit along one side of the Rapidan at the edge of our property where we would wade the swift, shallow current on slippery stones and bathe with homemade soap in the cold water. We used an outdoor john behind the house at dawn and before bedtime and kept a jar under the bed for midnight emergencies. We were poor, but I had no clue that we were. It was simply the way we lived and I knew nothing else. In fact, living on "The Farm," as we called the place thereafter in our lives, comprised some of my happiest memories, to accompany some bad ones too, of course.

Although Dad had a job in Charlottesville as an architectural draftsman, he wanted to embrace the life of a Gentleman Farmer and Mother wanted to live as Rousseau suggested, as a primitive would. And The Sow's Ear Farm, as Dad named it, fit the bill for primitive. But true to the French philosopher, we younger kids were in a blissful state. The river turned at one corner of the farm and a small creek that fed the river marked a third border. The mile-long dirt/mud road that led to our house was the other edge. The result was, we could not get lost. We were always on our land as long as we did not cross water or the road. My brothers and I spent long days especially in the summers exploring our world. We awakened early, breakfast being either some of Mother's homemade soda bread, which we loved, or some clabber milk from the cows that we allowed the neighbors to pasture on our land. We hated clabber milk, even with the fresh blackberries or honey. The sour flavor was too strong for our young taste buds. After breakfast, we had a few simple chores, and then we were gone, a peanut butter sandwich wrapped in wax paper shoved into the back pockets of our hand-me-down jeans. Shirts and shoes were not needed.

Behind our dilapidated house, Dad had planted a huge vegetable garden that gave us almost no food but ensured healthy deer, raccoons, and rabbits. We stayed out of the garden except when we had to weed it, which was all the more difficult because we could scarcely determine healthy weed from scraggly vegetable. When we went out to play, we usually took one of two routes. Often, we walked up the dirt road that served as our entranceway but once it came up to our back door went on past our house as an old logging and gravel road, wending its way at the edge of the woods to the old gravel pit along the river. Or we could head directly across the field down the path towards the well-spring, which was an old wooden barrel sunk into the ground where a spring burbled forth. Along the woodside logging road, across from the pine forest, were wild blackberries and great clumps of pawpaw trees. A tin-roofed shack was also along that road, maybe three rooms, the exterior covered in red, faux-brick asphalt siding. We seldom entered the Red House, as we knew it, perhaps because it was locked (we didn't test it that I recall), but perhaps because it was fairly overgrown and quite uninviting. We were allowed to swim up at the gravel pit, although swimming would be euphemistic since the water was shallow in most places. A few pools were deeper but not too much so. But on those summer mornings, we would usually first scramble down the well path to ride the buffalo rocks, large mounds of granite left by retreating glaciers thousands of years before. Across the footpath, juts of basalt were sharks, waiting to grab us as we tiptoed along the trail towards Lookout Pine, an eastern white whose branches made it almost like climbing stairs. Near the top, or as near the top as we ever climbed, two limbs branched out symmetrically from the trunk, allowing my one brother, Glen, two-years my senior, and I to sit there, partially hidden from view, and watch the other wild things of our woods pass by - wild turkey, deer, squirrels. When Dad came down to fetch water, we spied quietly on him, but his smirk made us think he perhaps had a clue where we were.

After a lunch of crushed sandwiches and pawpaws, washed down with fresh spring water cupped in our grimy palms, we would come back towards the house, making a left at the chicken coop before mother saw us and called us in for any chores she could find for us. That was when we went back along the blackberries and into the woods to explore. The woods were full of bandits and pirates and tigers, forcing us to fend them off with wooden sabers and stick guns. We swung on tendrils of cross vine into nets of honeysuckle, first one of us, then the other two. Red mulberries made for not only sweet treats, but left wonderfully realistic looking wounds on each other during our frequent battles. Before we went home, we slipped up to the river to wash off the dirt and sweat of another day's adventures, albeit haphazardly. We often swam alone there at the gravel pit, but we had been given dire warnings about swimming on the other side of the farm where the Rapidan curled to our north. According to local lore, there was the "Sixteen Foot Hole" there that swallowed up innocent swimmers, their helpless bodies forever pinned by the unnaturally twisted currents to two giant boulders that had been unartfully dislodged from the river bed by an explosion. The story was someone used dynamite to kill fish rather than rely on hooks and worms. That they knew even less about explosives than they did about fishing left a menacing legacy.

Our own river bathing rarely forestalled the evening bath, which usually included a somewhat rough scrubbing with what once had been a washcloth now covered with a sudsy film of lye soap. We needed the scrubbing, covered as we were in dirt and tree sap and grime. The ring of dirt around our neck - granny beads - always received a hard wash, leaving our necks clean, but a little raw. We usually had pointed out to us at that time the many bites and stings we had received during the day, although we were never slowed by such minor injuries. After baths, dinner was around the table in an almost formal way, each of us in our usual seat, taught table manners, and dining on hasenpfeffer made from Dad's hunting expedition earlier in the day or chicken cacciatore made from one of the very tough wild chickens we inherited at the farm.

If it sounds idyllic, it was to us. Although the house was literally falling down (the kitchen floor had given way and been propped up unevenly), and gave only the merest protection from the elements, we had a wonderland outside. We were so far from neighbors that we really only had each other as playmates. My older sister was in high school and had friends, and my oldest brother was in school as well, so had some friends. But Glen and I were fast buddies, made even more so by the fact I had a serious speech impediment that no one but Glen could decipher. I caught whooping cough while we lived there, which may have been the result of the drafty house as much as anything. While I was sick, my brothers slept downstairs. It was the only time I had my own room until my oldest brother went off to the army many years later.

We had a fellow who lived upstairs over the kitchen for a short while, a very slow-witted man whom mother had brought home from a soup kitchen in Charlottesville to do chores around the farm. He was hard-working but had a terrible time understanding the simplest instructions. He helped Dad build the chicken coop where the free-range and very rangy chickens had flown in to join Dad's small flock of laying hens. He helped hack away at the woods behind the house to broaden the field where Dad envisioned an orchard and he split slags of lumber left behind from some previous timbering on the land for our drum stove and for cooking. He helped us build a dam in the creek to create a small pool of very cold water that mother thought would be a better place to bathe, but the dam was not strong enough to hold past the first rain. So he had a willingness to work and he also provided adult supervision, such as it was, for us three boys, although it was under his watch that I piled all Glen's toys under a rocking chair (and he did not have a lot of toys) and lit them with a match, destroying his toys and the rocking chair, and leaving a deep burnt spot in the wooden floor. It is an absolute wonder the entire house did not go up in a puff. I should explain: the rocking chair was an old west wagon that needed blowing up. Glen's toys were evidently better suited for such pyrotechnics than my own. Although it's really quite reasonable, The Great Xylophone Fire remained a topic of contention for many years.

One day the hired man was just gone. I didn't know where he came from and I never knew where he went. In that way, he was a bit like the scraggly collie that turned up one winter morning, hungry and forlorn. I think the collie stayed around longer.

We did have animals. Dad had his chickens. And Bruce had a pig for a 4-H project. The pig was uncommonly resourceful at fleeing his pen despite Dad's numerous attempts to eliminate his escape routes, and when he escaped, he chased us kids all over the farm. I was terrified of the beast. Dad thought the pig chasing us around the yard was hilarious and he sat on the remnants of a front porch, laughing uncontrollably as he watched us squeal with terror, the porcine menace close on our heels. Then one day, the pig chased him. While we then saw how a person being chased by a barnyard animal could be funny, the pig too was simply gone one day soon thereafter. We had a small mixed terrier named Honey Bun. It was a motley little dog that ate whatever was placed before him: bones, salad, soured milk, whatever. He was a hunter too, often turning up with a rabbit in his mouth even when Dad did not. I never knew where the dog came from or where it ended up. One day, my older sister came home with a stray cat she named Johnny

B. Goode. The poor thing was terrorized by my brothers and me. I'm not proud of it – we simply didn't know how to treat a cat. I suppose I should have known tossing it in the air by its tail was not good treatment, though. But the cat took its own revenge by waiting at the edge of the path where the grass was taller heading towards the outhouse. When we ran by with full bladders, it would pounce, all teeth and claws. We learned to leave the cat alone.

My younger sister was born in that house, delivered by my father. We had been sent to the Colvin's for the day to get us out of the way, which was unusual enough to arouse our curiosity, and sure enough, we came home to a baby sister. She was tiny with a sweet disposition.

A few miles away, a tiny Baptist church, a picturesque little chapel, stood at the edge of a woods. A pole shelter protected a few picnic tables to one side. A cemetery rested behind the church. I remember going to Bible school there in the summer. We were not at all Baptist, but mother was not one to turn down free day care. We made popsicle stick ornaments with photographs of a very European Jesus glued in the middle and paper plate drawings of our hands. It was the usual vacation Bible school projects, but nonetheless, my recollection of that little church is a tender one.

When I turned six, I started school, which meant February. I don't know if it was the policy for children to start school the month they turned six or just my mother's insistence, but I was happy to go. The trek to the bus stop with my siblings was one for the books. The dirt road with the occasional stream to wade was nearly a mile long, and then we had to walk up the hill another mile. Then there was the long bus ride. We left and came home in darkness. But I was excited to go to school with my brothers and my older sister (although she stayed on the bus to be taken on to the high school).

My first teacher was Mrs. White. I have a clear recollection of her. She was quite elderly, although as a child, anyone over twenty-seven seemed middle-aged to me. But she had grey hair pulled back in a bun and wore faded-print dresses that ballooned around her. She didn't like my entering her class so late in the year, I suppose, but for whatever reason, she was never very fond of me, although there was a little girl who sat in front whom she doted on. Once, she decided I was turned too far around in my seat after returning from lunch and she shook me so hard my teeth clattered. When I told Dad about it, he told me to sit straight in my desk and try not to get into trouble. I understood then that adults are in cahoots. Each day at school, we could buy a popsicle at recess for a nickel, but for the longest time, I never had one. Mrs. White would ask each morning just before recess who had a nickel for a treat and kids all around me raised their hands (although by no means all of them) but I sat there, both wishing I could have a treat and embarrassed that I never had a nickel. I begged my Dad for a nickel, but he always told me he didn't have one. That was when I began to realize that we were poor. Every day I asked, and every day the answer was the same, and every day, Mrs. White asked who had money for a treat and I sat there dejected. Finally, one day I asked for a nickel and Dad surprised me by fishing one out of his pocket and handing it to me. I was so excited I gripped that nickel with all my might. Finally, I would get a popsicle and, perhaps as important, I would not have to sit there, embarrassed at my poverty and my sorry-for-myself attitude.

"Who has popsicle money today?" Mrs. White asked in a sing-song. My hand shot up. I was so proud to be able to raise my hand on the occasion I think I was nearly glowing. I waved my hand excitedly. "Larry?" Mrs. White walked towards me, her face a mix of contempt and pity. She held her hand out before her. "Hand me your nickel." In the many days preceding this, when treat-purchasing time arrived, she had not taken up the money in this way. I was baffled, but I handed Mrs. White my nickel. She turned around and walked back to the front of the classroom and handed my nickel to the little girl she doted on. "Here, honey. Now you have money for a snack." She patted the girl's back as she gave her my coin. I was devastated. My long-awaited treat was gone, given away to the teacher's pet for reasons I could not fathom, and still don't to this day. How could she have treated me that way? I was dejected the rest of the day, my young brain trying to sort out my injustice.

That night, as we sat around the dinner table, Dad beamed at me. "So, how was your snack today?" I told him the story reluctantly, sure that I had done something wrong, or else I would not have had my money taken away. I can still see Dad's face turn from smile to furrowed brow to scowl as I spoke. Dad ended up furious over the event and went to the next school board meeting. Evidently, caught up in my own little universe, I never noticed that Mrs. White had purloined a number of other children's nickels for the benefit of her pet. She didn't finish the year.

Hurricane Gracie paid us a visit in September of 1959. We had been forewarned she was a bad storm, and she delivered as promised. History says she was one of the worst to hit the east coast. I remember watching Dad drive through the gate just before it got really bad, and when he tried to close the gate, the wind lifted him off his feet. He left the gate open and came to the shuddering house and we all sat in the hallway, waiting for the house to be blown away. It didn't, but after the storm, our Sow's Ear Farm was a wreck and the road was nearly impassable for weeks. It was not long after that, we moved to Charlottesville, the gentleman farmer tired of the load of trying to work a day job and be a full-time farmer as well. I have returned to the farm a couple of times since and was even able to make a map of my recollection of where things were. My Scuffletown memories are mostly warm ones, the colder events, perhaps, relegated to the nether world of Best Left Forgotten.

Hasenpfeffer

Ingredients:
2 or 3 rabbits, cleaned and cut into pieces
1/2 teaspoon salt
1/3 cup all-purpose flour
1/2 pound bacon, diced
1 finely chopped onion
2 cloves garlic, minced
1 cup dry red wine
1 cup water
1 chicken bouillon cube
1 tablespoon currant jelly
15 black peppercorns, crushed
1 bay leaf
1/4 teaspoon dried rosemary
2 teaspoons cider vinegar
3 tablespoons water
2 tablespoons all-purpose flour
1/8 teaspoon dried thyme

Directions:

1. Place bacon in a large, deep iron skillet. Cook over medium high heat until evenly brown. Drain on paper towels and set aside. Sprinkle rabbit with salt and coat with 1/3 cup flour, shaking off excess. Brown rabbit in remaining bacon fat. Remove from skillet and reserve.

2. Sauté onion and garlic in skillet over medium low heat for about 4 minutes, until tender. Stir in wine, 1 cup water and bouillon cube and deglaze. Heat to boiling over medium high heat, then stir in jelly, peppercorns, bay leaf, and rosemary. Return rabbit and bacon to skillet. Heat to boiling, then reduce heat to low. Cover and let simmer about 1 1/2 hours or until rabbit is tender.

3. Remove bay leaf and discard. Place rabbit on a warm platter and keep warm while preparing gravy.

4. Stir vinegar into skillet with cooking liquid. Combine 3 tablespoons water with 2 tablespoons flour and mix together; stir mixture into skillet over low heat. Finally, stir in thyme. Pour gravy over stew and serve with egg noodles or spaetzle.

Chicken Cacciatore

Ingredients:
2 teaspoons olive oil
8 cloves garlic, sliced
2 (28 ounce) cans whole peeled plum tomatoes with juice
1 (6 ounce) can tomato paste
3/4 cup red wine
1 tablespoon white sugar
1 tablespoon dried oregano
1 tablespoon dried basil

1 teaspoon salt
1/2 teaspoon ground black pepper
2 tablespoons olive oil, divided
1 carrot, chopped roughly
1 stalk celery, chopped roughly
2 green bell peppers, cut into chunks
2 onions, cut into chunks
1 pound fresh mushrooms, sliced
½ cup green olives, sliced
½ cup black olives, halved
2 eggs
2 cups all-purpose flour
1/4 cup olive oil
1 large chicken, cut into pieces (When we were older, because we all preferred the dark meat, Dad used all leg quarters)
1 1/2 pounds dry spaghetti
1/2 cup chopped fresh parsley
Shredded Parmesan cheese

Directions:

1. Heat 2 teaspoons of olive oil in a large pot over low heat, and cook and stir the garlic until tender but not browned, about 3 minutes. Pour in the tomatoes with their juice, and mash with a potato masher to leave the tomatoes in chunks. Stir in tomato paste, red wine, sugar, oregano, basil, salt, and black pepper, and mix until the tomato paste is smoothly combined into the sauce. Bring to a simmer, and cook, stirring often, while you prepare the vegetables.

2. Heat 1 tablespoon of olive oil in a skillet over medium heat, and cook and stir the carrot and celery until tender, 5 to 8 minutes. Stir into the sauce. In the same skillet, cook and stir the green peppers and onions until the onions are translucent, 5

to 8 more minutes; mix them to the sauce. Heat 1 more table-spoon of olive oil in the skillet, and cook and stir the mush-rooms until they give up their liquid, about 10 minutes; stir the mushrooms into the sauce. Add the olives and allow sauce to simmer while you cook the chicken.

3. Beat the eggs in a bowl. Place the flour in a separate shallow bowl. Heat 1/4 cup of olive oil in a large cast iron skillet with deep sides over medium heat. (Dad had a huge cast iron skillet with a lid he used for this. If you don't have one, you can use a Dutch oven.) Dip chicken pieces in egg, then dredge in flour. Tap off any excess flour, and brown the chicken pieces in the hot oil until browned on both sides, about 15 minutes.

4. Preheat oven to 300 degrees F.

5. Pour sauce and vegetables over the chicken and stir to ensure sauce is also beneath the chicken; cover.

6. Bake in the preheated oven until the chicken is tender and no longer pink inside, about 1 hour.

7. Prepare the spaghetti noodles according to package instructions for al dente. Drain.

8. Turn the spaghetti out onto a large platter, and top with the chicken and sauce. Sprinkle with parsley and Parmesan cheese to serve.

Clabber milk (or clabbered milk)

When we were little, this relative of yogurt was far too sour for us. As an adult, I find it quite flavorful and it is very healthy. Clabber milk can be eaten in a bowl with fruit like one might eat yogurt, and it can be used in making baked goods as leavening. This is how I recall it being made at The Sow's Ear Farm using fresh raw milk we received as payment for allowing the cows to graze our fields or in barter with my mother for reading the tarot cards for the neighbor.

<u>Ingredients and directions:</u>

Pour 1 gallon fresh, raw milk into large canning jars. Place tops on loosely and store in a warm spot (ours was near the wood-fired cookstove). The cream will rise and clabber from the naturally occurring bacteria in the milk. Left long enough, it turns into cottage cheese.

Mother made bread with clabber milk, making a dough of white flour, baking soda, clabbered milk and salt. Then she would bake it in the wood-fired oven (roughly 350 degrees) for twenty to thirty minutes. She never measured but just added milk or flour until the dough was not sticky to the touch but still very moist. She used a baking sheet with the loaf free formed.

Grit

We were living in a tiny apartment in the back of a large old house on Daviess Street near Thirteenth Street. There were five of us in the three rooms, Dad, my younger sister, and me and my two older brothers. We had an old footlocker with a small television on it sitting before the tattered cast-off couch Dad was sleeping on. All of us kids slept in the lone bedroom, the boys on a double bed, my sister in a playpen from the Goodwill Store. Our oldest sister slept at our grandmother's, where she had been living for several years anyway. Dad had bought a ham knife and a huge ham which we ate in various forms for a week, always with potatoes or rice or noodles to help fill us up. With our meals, each child had a half glass of milk. We had only recently returned to Dad's hometown of Owensboro, and we had yet to get our feet fully under us. And we had very little.

My brother Glen was nine. I was seven. We were about the same size, and equally skinny, with a few hand-me-down clothes from our cousins in Texas and spikey butch haircuts. It was early autumn, and school had started, so we were kept busy during the week while Dad was out looking for work. Most weekends we spent galloping through the alley behind the house, climbing trees and throwing rocks in the air for the bats to chase when they came out at dusk. This particular Saturday, however, Glen, who was always industrious, decided he could make some money by selling Grit magazine. He had seen the advertisement in a Richie Rich comic book we read at Shown's Drugs before being chased out by the man behind the lunch counter. The ad had extolled the virtue of making money by going door to door selling America's Greatest Family Newspaper. There was even a suggestion that the millions Richie Rich's father enjoyed had begun with a stint selling the good news in Grit. What looked to me like a huge stack of papers were delivered to the house, showing up mysteriously one morning on the sidewalk that led to our tiny apartment. My brother had anticipated its delivery and eagerly snatched it up, carrying the bundle, tied together with twine that cut into his fingers, as he wagged the stack of journals by his side. I fell in along-side him and we went up and down Frederica Street, the four-lane main street in town, selling the good news magazine at the barber shop, the donut store, and the furniture store. We went to the fire station and the drugstore and the accountant's office and even tried the door of the liquor store, but it wasn't open yet. We crossed back and forth across the busy boulevard. Sales were very slow, but Glen was determined to make some money. Finally, we turned the corner by the Carnegie Library and walked the few blocks over to the A & P grocery by the light bulb factory. The A & P was familiar territory. We often accompanied Dad for his weekly shopping trips. I recall Dad in those days getting a shopping cart full of food, six or seven large brown bags full of groceries, for twenty-five dollars. We knew people who shopped there often got change, if they didn't write a check, and the magazine only cost a dime. It was the perfect selling spot. We were finally on our way to join Richie Rich.

My job was to keep an eye on the stack of magazines and to keep a look-out for the store manager. We were not at all certain we were allowed to sell outside the entrance. My brother was the salesman. He targeted the people leaving the store, figuring those were the most likely to have the change on them, and that they were already in a shopping mood, having considered whether to get the Spaghetti-Os or the Chun King Chow Mein dinner. Folks came out from the store through the automatic doors followed by the bagger pushing the cart full of groceries to their cars. My brother would approach them with a variety of pitches suggested by the sales guide that came with the magazine: "Buy a Grit? Only a dime!" "It's America's good news magazine! Still only a dime!" "It's America's greatest family newspaper! Want to buy a Grit?" But sales were still very slow. No one seemed interested in buying this fabulous paper, even for a dime. Perhaps they were thinking of the tip they were about to give the grocery clerk. Maybe they didn't know what an amazing bargain they could be getting. We couldn't figure it out. The store clerks came and went and barely shot us a glance. Then we noticed that not only were folks not buying a paper, they were avoiding us altogether, trying to hurry past without being pitched to. We looked at each other and shrugged. What could we do? We still had almost a full stack of papers, perhaps thirty or forty cents earned, and we had spent the entire morning. I took out a Grit paper and read the funny pages. We had taken turns sitting atop the small stack of papers while the other hawked papers. We grew bored. This was not going as planned. Getting rich was evidently harder than we thought.

I was ready to go home, defeated and still poor. But my brother was not deterred. He had an idea. What we needed was a way to get people's attention. We slipped around the front wall of the A & P and he pulled out a safety pin he had found on the street and stuck in his pocket, the way any boy does when he finds an unexpected treasure. He pulled his left arm out of his long-sleeved plaid shirt that hung on him like a sack anyway since it was a good two sizes too large. He put his arm behind his back and had me pin the sleeve up to the shoulder of the shirt. He pulled one side of his shirt tail out and let it droop by his waist. Then we returned to the stack of papers. I stood over by the wall and my brother parked himself next to the stack of America's Good News Magazine, his one "good" arm holding up a copy to the people who came out of the A & P. These folks who had brushed past us before now stopped, their faces painted with sympathy and sorrow at the horrible fortunes that must have befallen this bedraggled, maimed Grit sales boy, his clothes disheveled, his eyes filled with earnest entreaty. They bought papers. They bought papers for a dime and for a quarter with a "Keep the change." They dropped coins alongside my brother without picking up a paper. There were even dollar bills in the stack.

I watched in utter amazement. My brother was brilliant! Richie Rich, move over! We were rolling in money! Unfortunately, one of the baggers must have noticed the sudden dismembering of my brother's arm. The manager came out, took a look at my pitiful brother, and shook his head. He recognized us, of course. The manager went inside and called Dad who drove the couple of blocks over to retrieve us and the remaining Grit magazines, which still was substantial. He looked at his son, the one-armed Grit salesman, but I'm not sure his face was one of consternation or bemusement as he picked up the stack of papers and herded us home. Dad sent the remaining papers back to the publisher to keep us out of trouble, but it wasn't long before my brother was delivering TV Guide throughout the neighborhood.

Ham steak

Pop was a big fan of ham since it fed his large family for not very much money and he liked the flavor. This was a regular item on his rotation of menus. Serves 4-6

Ingredients:
Vegetable oil
1 large slice of ham, at least 1 1/2" thick
½ can frozen orange juice concentrate, thawed
½ cup brown sugar
¼ cup spicy brown mustard
1/8 t ground allspice
Dash ground cloves

Directions:
Heat oven to 350 degrees. Wipe a large heavy cast iron skillet (or any large baking dish) with a paper towel that has been moistened with vegetable oil. Place ham in skillet. Mix remaining ingredients in a bowl then spread across the ham. Bake for twenty to thirty minutes until heated thoroughly. Slice into pie-type pieces keeping the topping on and serve.

Sometimes, Dad would place rings of canned pineapple atop the ham, substitute the pineapple juice in the can for the orange juice concentrate in the topping and then spread the topping on.

Cheese Grits

From: *Bluegrass Winners* (A Cookbook) Serves 8.

Ingredients:
6 cups water
2 teaspoons salt
½ cup (1 stick butter)
3 eggs, well beaten
1 pound sharp Cheddar cheese, grated (4 cups)
1 ½ cups grits
1 to 3 cloves garlic, minced
Cayenne pepper to taste

Directions:
Bring water to a rapid boil with salt; gradually stir in grits with a fork. Cook until all water is absorbed. Stir in butter bit by bit; carefully add eggs, cheese, garlic and cayenne pepper. Put into a greased 2 ½ quart casserole; bake at 350 degrees for 1 hour and 20 minutes.

Note: This dish may be frozen before baking, then thawed and baked.

This isn't a dish Dad made, but one he often requested my late wife make when he came to dinner. It's great with ham.

Pray for Us, St. Ann

We moved to St. Ann Street in Owensboro when I was seven. Dad had tried to take us to Kansas City to live because he had a job and an old army buddy there, but we weren't there more than a couple of days before we ended up traveling back to Dad's home town, where he had family and friends. For a brief time, we lived in a tiny apartment carved out of the back of an antebellum home on Daviess Street (after a brief stint in The Rudd Hotel downtown), but then we moved the few blocks over to St. Ann. We lived there for only about six months or so, but it was an important time in our family because we were discovering a new family dynamic.

This new dynamic resulted from a number of changes in our lives. First of all, our mother wasn't with us. She had run off with us four younger children in Virginia only to abandon us in a hotel in Cincinnati and vanish. I don't know if Dad knew where she was, but we didn't. We were three boys and a little sister. My oldest brother Bruce was 12, then Glen at 9 and me at 7. Our baby sister Rhoda was three. In addition to the four of us (and Dad, of course), our older sister Ana was now living with us and that was also a bit new. She had been around us only occasionally my first few years, being sent off to live with some of my Dad's relatives. She was eleven years my senior and at that time was attending college in Owensboro while I started second grade at Longfellow Elementary. She became the baby-sitter in the afternoons when we returned home from school. But the most important change was that we were now a single-parent family, which in 1960 was unusual enough, but a single-parent family where the father is the parent was rare. Because we were just getting our grounding, that six months on St. Ann with the six of us was filled with a number of false starts. Some of that had to do with the fact that while Dad got a drafting position with an excellent architect in town, that meant he was working all day before he came home to fix dinner and take care of us. As a result, we had perhaps more unstructured time than some other kids we knew.

The thirteen hundred block of St. Ann Street is a mix of two-story small houses that followed either Victorian and Romanesque floor plans but at that time generally lacked the ornamentation more expensive houses might have had. They were built in the late 1800's and early 1900's and when we lived there, they were not so much charming as just old. Many of the Romanesque houses used tin siding to simulate the stone that would have been found in true Romanesque houses and our house was Victorian purely in the front porch and gable design. But the house was large enough for us, with three bedrooms and a bath upstairs and a room Dad turned into a fourth bedroom downstairs. There was a small back yard and smaller front yard. A gravel alley ran behind all the streets in that neighborhood and we spent countless hours running around in the alley and backyard of the house. Many of the houses had the same tired, woven-wire garden fences with scalloped tops across the back yard and small garages that were accessed from the alley. There were a number of other kids in the neighborhood, both on our block and along the street behind us, Allen Street. All in all, while it wasn't fancy, it wasn't at all a bad place to be.

The house on the corner, which faced Thirteenth Street then, was a much larger and fancier Queen Anne style house. It was three stories, I believe, with rounded roof lines and even a cupula atop the entrance. An older woman lived there, so we made many of the usual childhood assumptions about her, including that she was mean, a spinster, angry, hated children, and so forth. Perhaps she was even a witch. To add to our misconceptions of her was the fact that bats lived in the uppermost reaches of her imposing house, flying out at dusk to feast on the moths and assorted beetles that gathered below the street lamps. Each evening, we watched the twenty or so bats fly out and hunt around the street lights on our street. We learned from a neighboring boy the first week we were on St. Ann that bats would follow rocks thrown into the air near them. That sounded like a marvelous experiment and we had to try it out, of course. One dusky August evening, while Pop was preparing his concoction he called "Little Meat with Sauce Diablo," we unsupervised three boys decided to find out the truth about bats and rocks. My two brothers and I gathered piles of gravel from the alley behind the house, stretching out our faded tee shirts to cradle as large a load as we could. It promised to be a great adventure with bats. We waddled our armaments to the front yard and stood on the sidewalk before our house, our tee shirts bulging with ammunition, our arms cocked, waiting for bats.

As if on cue, we watched the bats sweep out of the attic of the old lady's house and begin darting around the street lamps, changing direction at phenomenal speed. They whizzed past light poles and trees. They dipped. They soared. It should have been entertainment enough, but we had to try the bat-chasing-rock experiment. I threw first, a sorry toss, I confess, that came nowhere near the altitude of the bats but did manage to land on top of our faded red Buick station wagon. Although the rock was not large (it did fit my small hands), it landed with a much louder "thunk!" than we expected. Glen shot me a look to say, "You want to ruin the experiment? Stop!" Glen threw next, reaching back and letting go with a high arching toss that cleared the cars and came perilously close to the street lamp itself before disappearing in the dusky light, a bat hot on its trail. We were delighted! The experiment worked! Bats chase rocks! Who knew? We were in for an evening of adventure. I had another rock ready and so did Glen, but it was Bruce's turn. He was a sinewy kid with surprising strength to go with his agility. When he let go of the rock, it sped so quickly into the fading light, we only saw it take off from his hand and head straight up the street. We could have never known if a bat caught the rock in its sonar and followed it because he threw it so far. The crash of the breaking glass in the old woman's upstairs window told us the rock had indeed travelled well. We looked around at each other in panic, the sounds of tinkling glass still trailing down the street. Had we incurred the anger of the wicked old woman? Would she know it was us? We were surely doomed! What would be worse, the old woman casting some hideous curse on us, or our father's wrath when he found out? Neither option was good and we didn't wait to find out. We dropped our rocks from our tee shirts and ran around the house and in through the back door. We tumbled onto the floor in front of our hand-me-down, black and white television and nervously watched Marshall Dillon chase down a stage coach robber. Our clothes and bodies were filthy. Dad was making the gravy while the big pot of rice steamed next to him. I could smell the Worcestershire. He paid little attention to our arrival. When dinner was ready, he shooed us upstairs to clean up and we scrubbed our hands and faces in silence, cutting looks at each other but afraid to even acknowledge our crime. We sat unnaturally quiet throughout the evening, waiting for the knock on the door or phone call that would probably destroy our lives. When Dad asked us about our day, we murmured vague statements between "Nothing" and "We played in the backyard" (which meant we could not be throwing rocks in the front yard – a brilliant ruse!) But we still expected to be caught. It was a waste, really, so young, to be sent to prison for the felony of breaking windows, or, worse, turned into lizards for the old woman's viewing pleasure. But no knock or call ever came. I guess Dad never found out, and no children went missing from the neighborhood having been turned into toads, so we never learned what repercussions might have come from The Great Bat Experiment, but we were at least quick learners. We never threw rocks at those bats again, and we even avoided that end of the block, just in case an ambush awaited us there. You never know how devious a witch might be.

Across the alley lived a boy who was my age. He and his mother lived in one of the huge Victorian houses on Allen Street. He was an only child and didn't seem to mesh well with the other kids up and down the alleyway, but to Glen and me, he was just another potential playmate when we met him. He had a very active imagination and I recall him later being in my class. One day early in the school year, he was squinting ferociously at our teacher, Ms Cosler, who asked him what he was doing.

"I'm disintegrating you," he said in a low, raspy voice.

"Well, stop disintegrating me and get back to work," Ms Cosler said with a smile. I think she found his imagination, however misplaced, amusing.

The first and last time we played with the boy, he came down the alley with a small box in his hands. We stopped building the dirt roads for our tiny cars and asked him what he had.

"Magic powder." His attitude was a bit smug, as it should be if you possess magic anything.

We were immediately intrigued, naturally. "What's it do?" Glen asked, peering into the box. It looked an awfully lot like Nestles chocolate milk mix.

"It makes me invincible!"

"Wow. Really?" I wanted some and stepped forward, but he pulled the box away and stepped backwards a step. He took one hand and scooped out a big pinch and swallowed it down, then stood in front of us, his chest puffed up like a superhero from a comic book.

"Huh. So, now you're invincible?" Glen was dubious.

"Yep!"

So Glen socked him in the eye.

The little boy dropped his magic powder on the ground, clamped his hand over his already mousy eye, and ran home crying, as much from the failure to become invincible as the pain, I think. Glen shrugged, looked at me, and we went back to our civil engineering work.

Glen and I were almost exactly the same size, but he was always the older brother and often led me into trouble or kept me out of it, depending on the circumstances. One afternoon, Johnny, a boy two doors down, showed up with a bb gun. It was an impressive weapon, black metal with just a bit of the paint scraped off. It had a cocking action that was used to build up air pressure, and the vaguely maple wooden stock was showing some wear, but we had never shot a gun of any sort, so this was an amazing new item. We stood in the dust of our once grassy front yard (we were hard on lawns, through sheer numbers), with only cutoff shorts on. It was warm and muggy. When Johnny arrived, all attention was on the air rifle. First, Johnny shot at paper cups we found in the gutter. Then, Glen shot small stick houses we built in the dusty yard, watching them scatter in a sudden blast of copper coated lead. I was waiting my turn anxiously. But my brother wasn't done. He shot at the fence that ran across the side yard, making the metal posts ping. He shot tin cans salvaged from the burn pile in the back yard. By that point, I think he was tired of inanimate targets. He turned, looked at me, and said, "Take off!"

"What?" He pointed the gun in my direction.

"Run!" Terrified, I took off at a gallop, but I only made it a few steps before I heard the bb gun give out its "Tump!" and the searing pain of a gunshot wound tore through my belly. Okay, it actually only made a small dent in my skinny tummy, but nonetheless I had been shot! Gut shot! By my brother! Whose crazy idea was it to arm him in the first place?

I ran down St. Ann Street, up a block to Frederica Street, then all the way out to the office where our Dad worked, which was on the 2600 block. I made the mile in no less than twenty-five minutes, in my bare feet and cutoffs, my hand held tight over my injured stomach. I stumbled into the office where Dad worked to show him the terrible deed, sure that this injustice would not go unpunished. I am certain I stumbled in the same way I had seen injured cowboys stumble into The Ponderosa. He took one look at me, his filthy child embarrassing him at his new job, and snatched me up and down the steps in a quick single motion. He drove me home in silence. I, of course, whined incessantly about my crippling injury that he took a quick glance at and then ignored. We stopped in front of our house (the culprit had long since made his escape) and he reached across and opened the door. "Go inside. Take a bath." I was confused. Where was the outrage? Where was the furious punishment for my attacker? "Go on." I got out and dragged myself into the house.

That night, Dad fumed in the kitchen while he prepared a veal roast with lardons. I had embarrassed him at work. Over dinner, he told us solemnly he had been fired from his job because his family wouldn't behave and was too much of a distraction for him. It wasn't true that he had been fired, but he made his point, and we understood a little better at that point that we were all in this together. However, I don't think Glen was even yelled at for committing wanton brother shooting. There is no justice.

But then I was no angel, so perhaps it all evens out. One Saturday morning Glen and I went outside early while Dad fixed eggs with a hat. We climbed into Dad's Buick. We pretended to drive all over town, or at least what little we knew of it at that time. We took turns, first Glen, then me, driving to faraway destinations and being very "Dad-like." "If I have to stop this car." "You kids stop fighting!" We knew the dialog better than actors on the stage. "Who wants ice cream?"

Maybe because we were being Dad-like is why I pushed in the cigarette lighter that all cars then were equipped with. More amazing is that even with no key, the lighter heated up to a bright orange-red and popped back out for me. I pulled it out and burned my finger a bit but held on long enough to discover that red hot lighters can make fascinating artwork on vinyl seats. Oh the artistry! First, there was a line of circles, then overlapping circles. Then circles in a square pattern, sort of. When the lighter cooled off, we pushed it back in the hole. The glorious scent of melting vinyl filled the car. Glen joined in – circles that went up the middle of the seat. Circles along the edge. Circles everywhere. It was a splendid sight.

When Dad came out to get us for breakfast, for some reason, he did not get our art. His face was rather one of total shock and dismay. And then maybe a little defeat. He sent us in to wash up, still staring at the wondrous art work. Funny thing is, I don't recall him ever saying much about it.

I was the usual hapless kid then. Once, I was engaged in a major excavation project in the side yard there on St. Ann that involved digging furiously for hours with an eight inch length of galvanized pipe I had found in the alley. I discovered it was a very adequate digging tool and managed to dig several inches deep before I ran into some roots from the maple tree that stood in the back yard. But I refused to be defeated by roots, since I had a real tool at my disposal. Besides, the roots weren't all that large by the time they had wound through the clay over to the side yard, so the pipe became a multi-purpose piece of heavy equipment. What a great find! I dug beneath the root with the galvanized wonder and then started using the fulcrum power of the steel pipe to pull upwards on the root. Unfortunately, my plan worked. The root broke; the pipe converted its potential energy into kinetic energy until it hit me square in the forehead. I was out cold. I awoke to find myself with a terrific headache, lying next to a stupid hole in the ground with a worthless piece of pipe lying in the bottom of it. I considered crying and running for attention, but then I remembered Dad had gone to the grocery, so I went in and watched Mickey Mouse Club and rubbed the sizeable knot on my forehead. Dad asked me about it when he got home, but for some reason, he found my injuries comical. I think it maybe had to do with the cigarette lighter in the car, but I can't be certain.

I also knocked my brother out during that stretch of time, unloading lumber Dad had bought to build some shelves on the back porch. It really wasn't my fault he was leaning over to pick up some boards at the very time I dropped some more on the stack. He lay on the stack for several seconds before coming to, long enough for me to hurry and see if Dad needed any assistance in the back yard. Dad sold that station wagon not long after that. I remember his taking one of the one hundred dollar bills the buyer had given him and lighting a cigarette with it before quickly extinguishing the burning Ben Franklin. I think he may have gotten more money because of the beautiful seat decorations we had made.

It was a small miracle we did not cause greater physical injury to ourselves or others on St. Ann. It was while we lived there that we saw the recently released movie The Magnificent Seven. Glen, Bruce and I loved how the gunslingers had booby trapped the village, so we booby trapped the back yard. We had holes we had dug throughout the yard covered with branches, strings tied tautly at face level (for two skinny boys), even hiding places for us to ambush the evil Calvera. If we had had that bb gun, we would have been fully prepared, but I was not sorry the gun did not reappear.

We got to see a number of movies that summer due to a promotion Malco Theater and Royal Crown Cola had where we could go see a Saturday matinee with the presentation of six RC Colas tops. Dad never bought colas so we tied a magnet to a piece of string and went over to the Conoco Gas station around the corner and fished out bottle caps from the soda machine. The owner didn't care and as the summer progressed, there seemed to be more RC Cola caps in the bin than before so he may have actually supported our movie going. Even as a young child, the advent of the Saturday matinee made we wonder why the movie owners did it. The house was packed with screaming, wild kids who threw popcorn boxes and spilled drinks and made an incredible mess. But we got to see The Sword of Sherwood Forest, Comanche Station, and The Time Machine, along with shorts by The Three Stooges and Our

Gang. We rarely had money for snacks, but I don't recall feeling neglected for it. We always had fun and never minded the ten block walk each way to see the movie. Bruce and Ernie and I went every Saturday. Occasionally, we would save our allowance money (25 cents a week) to go to a horror movie. I remember running home with Bruce, both of us at full sprint after watching The Brides of Dracula that fall. Once, Dad took all of us to the Centre Theatre to see Old Yeller. We all bawled so loudly Dad took us home.

Just after Labor Day, I started second grade at Longfellow Elementary School. Recess was always an adventure, at least it remains so in my memory. It was only a few days into the school year when I was swinging on the chain and strap swing set, going so high, the chains would snap just a bit as they gained a tiny bit of slack at the top. When the bell rang to end recess, I made up my mind to jump off at the end of the swing, just to satisfy my appreciative audience. I did allow myself to slow from my peak swing, but then I launched myself toward the sky and landed pretty much on all fours, with just a bit of an "oof!" for emphasis. When I looked around for my thunderous applause, no one was there (the bell had rung, after all) except the school bully James. James was fourteen in the fourth grade. I have no idea what his life was like, so I pass no judgment, but I remember that he was very angry very often and that he was too old for the fourth grade. But this was before social promotions so there he was, glowering at me because my rapidly vacated swing had swung back and brushed against him as he walked past the swing set. He was on me before I could gain my breath and run, and he was flailing. I screamed (I know it was a manly scream) and Glen, also a fourth grader, looked down the hill and saw James punching away on me. Glen raced down Longfellow Hill and took a full uppercut that caught James square on the chin and sent him rolling off of me. Glen glanced at James, who was a foot taller than Ernie and outweighed him by thirty pounds, then back at me.

"Run!" Glen picked me up and we scampered up the hill and inside before James could get his feet.

We were marched to the principal's office, Ms Perguson, whom we lovingly referred to as Miss Percolator, although I came to know when I was old enough to be aware of such things that she was a truly remarkable educator. She was very stern and quite unhappy with us for fighting, but when Glen explained what happened, she began to nod her head and purse her lips and eventually we were sent back to class without any punishment. James was not seen at Longfellow afterwards.

As I mentioned before, my second grade teacher was Ms Cosler and I adored her. She was very kind and tender towards me. I loved going to school there at Longfellow. It was a wonderful, solid WPA-era brick building atop Longfellow Hill. We had recess out the back door and down the hillside to the playsets. There were swings and climbing sets and monkey bars (which were reserved for third grade and higher), a big open field, and ball diamonds. I made fast friends with Tommy, who was a good deal bigger and the only kid faster than I in second grade at Longfellow Elementary. We often chose to be teammates in kickball or racing. One weekend soon after the fight with James, a storm blew down one of the huge oaks that stood on top of the hill which flattened the (to me) very tall chain link fence that kept children in the playground and others out. Tommy and I were hiding behind the enormous tree for no other reason than we were seven years old and there was a huge tree lying there when the bell rang signaling the end of recess. We crouched behind the still green leaves of the fallen giant, watching our classmates line up to go back in. We were about to pop up and run to get in line when we realized no one seemed to be missing us. We gave each other a glance then slouched lower behind the tree trunk. After a few minutes, the playground was quiet. We peeked back over the tree and everyone had gone inside. This was something new. We were free! Tommy and I sneaked over the downed fence and up McCreary Avenue where Tommy lived. We spent the next several hours eating toast and playing at his house and feeling remarkably guiltless. When we looked at the clock and saw school would be letting out soon, we slipped down the street, over the fence and fallen tree, and back into the school to line up with the kids just letting out. We thought we were diabolical geniuses for the level of the sneakiness we had pulled off until Ms Cosler caught sight of me and nearly fainted. Turned out she had been frantically searching for me, for some reason. Once again, we were taken to Ms Perguson's office and this time, she was not happy with Tommy or me. When Dad came in, called yet again to tend to his wayward seven-year-old, he was very, very unhappy, but all he said to Ms Perguson was that he would handle it, which she accepted readily and which thus terrified me. I may have gotten a spanking, but I don't really remember that. I do remember hearing about the dangers I had unwittingly faced, from kidnappers to murderers and such, which did scare me. That night, Dad made Welsh Rarebit, telling us again the story how the German grandmother, Mother Weill, made rarebit and the English grandmother, Mother Pruitt, demurred because it had beer in it. Thereafter, Mother Weill made two batches of Welsh Rarebit, which was the big pan of cheese fully prepared, then a portion scooped out and falsely labelled as beer-free. Throughout dinner, Pop kept looking at me and shaking his head in dismay.

About a week later, during recess, the tree having been removed, I decided prohibitions against second graders using the monkey bars was unnecessarily hindering my freedom, so I climbed up the end of the playset and reached up and gripped the first bar. I could barely reach it and my grasp was tenuous, but I was on a mission. I let go of the side and lurched up and grabbed the bar with both hands. I was ready. I swung my wispy body forward to allow me to progress across the monkey bars, immediately lost my grip and fell in a small mangled mess at the foot of the ladder. I untangled myself, brushed the dust off of my hand-me-down clothes (actually, they had been handed down from cousins to my brothers before coming to me), and tried to stand proudly as if to declare, "I meant to do that," although, of course, everyone knew better. My left arm hurt rather badly, but I didn't want to let on, so I held it closer to my side, which seemed to help, and tried my best to saunter confidently to the line to go in from recess. My forearm ached fiercely by the time I got inside and had a funny bruise across the middle. I went up to Ms Cosler and told her I hurt my arm, but she was suspicious of me after my skipping school escapade and told me to stop whining and go back to my seat. I sat in quiet pain the remainder of the school day, then went home and went to bed. I didn't cry over it (it was my own fault after all – so that's why only third grade and above are allowed on the monkey bars!) but I didn't feel like playing, so my sister knew something was up. When Dad came home after work, he took one look at my s-curved arm and nearly fell over. It was pretty ugly by then.

When I showed up at school the next day with my cast, poor Ms Cosler broke into tears. She apologized repeatedly and I loved her all the more for it. I was, of course, a celebrity among my classmates because of the injury, so I didn't regret the adventure on the monkey bars as much as I probably should have, although they remained my nemesis for several years.

One warm autumn Saturday, I found myself playing alone in the backyard and felt rather sad. My brothers had gone to a birthday party and I wasn't invited. It's true, the boy whose birthday it was was three years older than I but my brothers were my playmates, and I didn't like the feeling of being left out. I moped around in the backyard for a bit, then went inside to see if my sister Ana wanted to do something fun, but she was studying and couldn't play. The more I requested that she find me something fun to do, the more irritated she became until she finally yelled at me to go outside and stop pestering people.

So that was it. I was only a pest. Dad had gone to the A&P with my baby sister to do the shopping, a great outing I was no longer invited to since I had once managed to take his very full grocery cart too fast around a corner and emptied everything onto the floor of the grocery store. It wasn't fair. No one loved me. I decided they would be very sorry they had left me out if they no longer had me around to be mean to. I decided I had to strike out on my own. If they didn't need me, I didn't need them. I took one of my Dad's handkerchiefs and wrapped up all I would need (I had seen how hobos did that on television shows). I had an extra tee shirt, a somewhat mushed up peanut butter and jelly sandwich wrapped in a huge strip of aluminum foil, and a jar once used for maraschino cherries now filled with water. What else could I possibly need? I tried to tie the bundle to a stick to carry on my shoulder but couldn't figure that one out, so I just carried my roll instead. I headed out, slipping through the backyard to the alley way, then up to Lewis Street where a set of train tracks ran down the middle of the street heading to the grain and gravel businesses downtown. I would hop a freight. It's what the hobos all did when they left their troubles behind. I had never actually seen a train on these tracks (I found out when I was older they almost always used these loading spurs only at night) and I was not sure how one goes about actually climbing aboard a moving train, but I was ready.

I stood on the corner of Lewis and 13th for a while but no train came. Undeterred, I started off on foot. I walked along Lewis for a block, then another. I was still grousing in my mind the injustices I had suffered. Eventually, I found myself at the bridge that crosses the Ohio River. I had walked pretty far for a seven year old. I decided against heading across the bridge, opting instead to walk down to the riverfront. This was downtown, and there was plenty of traffic, but I knew to wait for the lights and I navigated my way to the green space there at the river. It's a lovely spot. I sat on the bank, ate my peanut butter sandwich that was dampened by water sloshing out of my cherry jar and drank the few gulps left in it. I sat watching the water flow by, looked at a barge passing through, counted birds, looked for shapes in the clouds, looked at my sneakers, got bored. It turned out, I had no idea what you do when you run away after you are finished running (or walking). I walked over by the ramp that led to the water, but it was just a big patch of concrete. I looked for rocks to throw into the water, but I wasn't very good at throwing and gave it up. I decided the birthday party was probably over, so I started home to play with my brothers. The walk home was far longer than the angry walk away, and by the time I made it home, I was pretty tired. I dragged myself through the backyard, threw my water jar and foil into the burn pile, and walked pitiably into the house. Dad was just unloading the groceries and my brothers, whom he had picked up on the way home, were upstairs changing into play clothes. Ana came in and asked

Dad if she could help put away the groceries, and he accepted. Everyone carried on as if I had not nearly been lost to them forever. I watched them going through these actions as if they didn't care I had run away. Then I realized no one had even missed me. My grand gesture was a grand failure. Glen came in and he and I went out to play in the backyard. I decided not to tell anyone that I had been gone. I saw no good coming from confessing I had run away.

That night, we had charcuterie (okay, we had cold cuts and pickles and mustard). Dad was always fond of Braunschweiger (I still am) and he had bought a big roll of it at the store. The meats and cheeses were arranged on a cutting board that we passed around the table. When Bruce passed the cutting board to Pop, he inadvertently tilted it ever so slightly, causing the Braunschweiger to roll to the end of the board, fly off, and land squarely in the middle of Dad's freshly brewed cup of coffee, sending the brown liquid flying everywhere. I don't think Dad would have been so upset if we hadn't all immediately broken into hysterical fits. It really was a perfect hit. He reached for the lunch meat, fumbled with the coffee cup for a moment, then stood abruptly and stormed out. He was gone for quite a while, and when he came back, he said he went out for a cup of coffee, but I knew what he had done – he had run away and gotten bored, I'll bet.

It was just a few weeks later when That Night occurred. Dad would tell and retell the story of That Night at our insistence. It started out, I was taking a bath, and discovered that when the shower curtain is on the inside of the tub while one is bathing, it is possible to plaster the curtain against the inside of the tub using nothing more than water. Even more impressive was the fact that if one left a fair amount of slack in the curtain before plastering it, it was possible to make a pouch that you could then fill with water and the curtain remained stuck. I was curious just how much water it could hold without failing so I continued to scoop water into the pouch until I found out that maximum amount was one less scoop of water than what I had just tried. Of course, water went everywhere, running across the floor and under the door and out into the hallway. Dad opened the door to my very stunned face and naked, still not washed body. He grabbed towels and mopped up the water, although it hardly seemed necessary since it was seeping readily though the many cracks in the linoleum floor. He just kept shaking his head and mopping up the water. After he had gotten me out of the tub (the scrubbing seemed a bit more rigorous than usual) and put me to bed, he finally found a moment to relax. He was lying in bed reading, waiting for Ana to come home from her date. She was perhaps a little late, so he was both sleepy and anxious, but eventually he heard the front door open and heard her climb the creaky stairs. Good. She's home. He allowed himself to drift off to sleep, but then he heard one of Ana's shoes hit the wood floor. He started awake. Okay. He waited for the other shoe to clump onto the floor, but it didn't. He finally fell asleep. In the middle of the night, he was awakened to screams from the makeshift bedroom below. He ran downstairs and found Glen covered in plaster. As it turns out, the lathe and plaster ceiling could not handle the amount of water that had seeped through the floor. Glen told me later he dreamed someone was throwing books at him. I can still picture the huge scar in the ceiling, a few remaining jagged chunk hanging precariously over the bed. Dad gave up, made a pot of coffee and stayed up the rest of the night.

Soon thereafter, Dad married the first of our step-mothers, a woman he had known in high school. She worked in an office, so we had more income. We moved from St. Ann Street to a bungalow on 22nd Street. It was a better place, with a bigger yard and an endless supply of children, and the ceilings were all intact.

Little Meat with Sauce Diablo

Serves 6
Ingredients:
2 pounds ground beef
1 onion, chopped
14 ounces beef broth
1 teaspoon salt
1 teaspoon garlic powder
2 tablespoons Worcestershire sauce
1 teaspoon pepper
1 teaspoon ground mustard seed
1 tablespoon butter, softened
1 tablespoon all-purpose flour

Directions:
Brown the ground beef and drain. Add onion and sauté until translucent. Add next five ingredients and simmer for 20-25 minutes, stirring occasionally. Knead together the flour and butter until smooth and add to the meat mixture, stirring to combine. Simmer until thickened. Serve over mashed potatoes or rice.

Veal Roast with Lardons and Potatoes

Serves 6
Ingredients:
1 large veal roast
1 white onion, chopped
2 cloves of garlic, sliced
½ pound thick cut bacon
1 cup dry white wine
Black pepper (to taste)
14 ounces beef stock
3 tablespoons sour cream
6 large potatoes, sliced

Directions:
Preheat oven to 250 degrees. Poke several shallow holes in the roast and fill with garlic slices. Brown the roast on all sides and remove the roast to a Dutch oven. In the same pan, fry over medium heat the potatoes, the bacon lardons and onion and cook until the lardons are just crisp.

Pour everything into a large Dutch oven over the roast. Add stock, white wine, pepper and sour cream.

Bake uncovered for 90 minutes, basting the roast occasionally with pan liquids.

Eggs with a hat

(I have seen a dozen different names for this one – totems, frog in a log, egg toast, and so on.) Serves 1

Ingredients:
1 slice white bread
1 egg

Directions:
Take a juice glass or small biscuit cutter and cut the center out of the bread. Place the bread and the bread center into a lightly buttered pan and fry until one side is just starting to brown. Flip the toast and the "hat". Crack the egg into the center of the bread and cook until the egg is set. Flip the toast and egg, put the hat on top of the egg portion to help hold the heat, and cook to desired doneness (about another 2 minutes for over medium).

Welsh rarebit

Serves 6
Ingredients:
12 slices pumpernickel bread
3 tablespoons butter, softened
1 tablespoon all-purpose flour
1/2 beer, preferable a stronger ale
1/4 cup whole milk
1 teaspoon dry mustard
1/8 teaspoon black pepper
1 ½ cups shredded extra-sharp Cheddar cheese

1 large egg yolk, beaten slightly

Directions:

Preheat broiler.

Spread one side of bread slices with butter, arrange slices buttered sides up on a baking sheet and broil 6 inches from heat until just toasted, about two minutes.

Melt 1 tablespoon butter in a heavy saucepan over low heat. Add flour and cook, stirring constantly, 1 minute. Add beer and milk in a stream, stirring constantly, then stir in mustard, pepper, and cheese. Bring to a simmer over moderately low heat, stirring, then simmer, stirring frequently, until smooth, about 2 minutes.

Remove from heat and immediately whisk in yolk. Serve cheese sauce on toast. Drink the remaining beer.

A Cackle of Children

It was 1961 when we moved from St. Ann Street out to 22nd street. Dad had remarried, this time to a woman he had known when they were both in high school many years before. The word was she had had a terrible crush on him back in school. Their courtship now being so fast was perhaps due to a combination of her longstanding affection for him and his seeing someone who could help him care for his rather large family he found himself suddenly caring for alone. That the marriage was ill-fated was also likely a result of their quick romance. But in the meantime, things changed rapidly for us.

First off, we moved from the small Queen Anne knockoff on St. Ann Street to a somewhat larger bungalow-style house out near one of the several parochial schools in Owensboro. I mention that because the neighborhood was packed with large families looking to be near the children's school. Twenty-second street is a decidedly residential boulevard with a wide island along the middle with maple trees and grass. It is very serene and inviting, at least until the children awaken. The house we lived in was a fairly standard bungalow with a concrete porch across three-fourths of the front replete with a porch swing and concrete bannisters and columns. The front yard had two gnarled maple trees and a scratchy yard that would soon become a virtual dust pile from our playing in it constantly. A narrow walkway around the east side of the house led to a back side door to the kitchen and, now using stepping stones, on around into a large backyard. Along that property line down the side of the house were sweetgum and wild cherry and redbud trees. An alley of crushed limestone marked the rear boundary and a scruffy wire picket fence with a brace of spirea marked the west property line. Parallel to the edge of the corner of our house, the wire picket fence gave way to a fence made from a cable stretched between pipes in the ground. The neighbors on the west side were elderly sisters whom we rarely saw. They kept to themselves, perhaps to keep from being inundated by children. They spread tobacco stalks around the front yard to encourage grass to grow but the intense shade of the maple trees made it a difficult proposition. To our east was an older couple whom we would see sitting on their porch swing occasionally. Next to them lived Poinsianna, my younger sister's new best friend. Inside our house, the first room was the living room with a fireplace at one end. I don't know if the fireplace worked, but we never had a fire, although we did hang stockings there at Christmas. The dining room was to the right behind the living room, the master bedroom on the left. Behind that were the very small kitchen on the right and a bath and hallway on the left that led to two more bedrooms. A set of stairs in the kitchen led to a basement.

The neighborhood was filled with children. Two doors down was a family with six children. Across the street was a family with ten children. On the next block was a family with seven children. We all played together and ran around like a pack of wild hyenas, running, jumping, chasing, fighting, and laughing. The lawns of every family with children were rutted from play. We were admonished to leave the neighbors who did not have children alone, I think because they simply wanted to have a lawn. The children from the catholic families attended Our Blessed Mother School, two blocks down 22nd Street. The rest of us went to Longfellow School, six blocks up on Frederica Street.

Pop began building a playhouse for us at the rear of the property. I believe he originally intended for it to be his drafting studio, but that never materialized. The basis of the building was an assembly of four wooden loading docks that were being discarded at Texas Gas Transmission Corporation, where my stepmother worked as a secretary. Dad built a simple frame from 2x4's and attached the docks vertically as walls. The docks had gaps for vehicles to sidle up to the loading area which became windows in our playhouse. He made rafters from 2x2's and lay plywood atop those, then large sheets of flattened cardboard boxes. There was a small line of redbud trees along the front. I don't know if Pop planted those of if they simply volunteered after he had levelled the dirt, but they made the little house seem even more special. He had plans to put tar paper on top, a door, some simple windows, but it remained in that partially finished state thereafter. We kids found it perfect. It was a fort in sweetgum ball fights (that often ended up as rock fights since gravel was readily available in the alleyway). It was a secret hideout from bandits that roamed through our imagination. It was a shop where we sold vegetables we invented from weeds in the yard: plantain seeds were asparagus; their leaves were spinach; pokeberry seeds were blueberries. And the little playhouse was also a quiet place to sit alone sometimes when we would tire of the constant rabble we were a part of and simply sit in what meager relief the playhouse provided from heat or cold and talk amongst ourselves, Bruce, Glen and I.

We had moved in the summer and quickly were immersed in the scene. Glen and I dug roads in the dirt, tearing up what little grass was left in the yard to pave the way for our small steel cars and trucks. We made tiny log homes from carefully snapped twigs and sat in the dust, our imaginary citizens in our imaginary town holding quiet conversations using our own whispered voices. I grew my first garden there in that back yard against the wire picket fence just beyond an out-of-control forsythia bush, a small patch of Big Boy tomatoes and a few radishes that struggled to gain girth in the hard ground. I loved watching the plants grow and that enjoyment has not abated. All in all, we were happy kids on 22nd Street. It's true, Glen took me snipe hunting at Blessed Mother School and when I didn't return, he grew worried, but I had simply taken up the offer of an old woman who saw my plight and brought me inside for cookies and hot chocolate. And we occasionally got into fist fights with the other neighborhood children over real and imagined slights and injuries. But mainly, we played. We played red rover and Simon says and redlight-greenlight. We played hide and seek with the giant maple tree in front as home base. We captured June bugs and tied thread to a foot and let them circle us in the muggy summer heat. We chased lightning bugs and played baseball with tennis balls and broom handles in the middle of Allen street, the cross street two doors down. The familiar yell of "Car!" interrupted play only momentarily and imaginary runners returned to the base they had formerly occupied imaginarily. We learned to walk on the painted street markings to keep from burning our bare feet on the blacktop made griddle by the August sun. The ice cream truck came around each afternoon, and now we actually received a meager allowance so, if we chose to, an orange push-up was ours on a steamy summer afternoon. We ran with abandon, with my older sister in charge since both Dad and our stepmother were at work, but most of the other mothers at that time in that neighborhood stayed home, so eyes kept a surprisingly careful watch over the packs of children. More than once, some minor infraction I committed was reported that evening to my Dad, who punished me accordingly, albeit not harshly.

Now that we had two incomes, Pop enjoyed expanding his menus. It was here on Twenty-second Street that he acquired a pressure cooker using S&H green stamps he received each week at the A&P. One of his favorite recipes with his new pressure cooker was a pot roast with a gravy thickened with ginger snaps. This was also where he made beef heart stew with noodles, which we were suspicious of for obvious reasons, but we found we liked a lot.

We had other distractions in addition to the hordes of children, including the fact that our new step mother was a member of Lakeside Country Club across the river in Rockport, Indiana. She and Pop would take us over the blue bridge and drive us the nine miles to the club so we could swim at the beach that was on one side of a lake at the edge of the club. We swam there frequently, splashing unartfully along the rope that cordoned off the area that non-swimmers should not go into. While Dad and his wife played golf and drank cocktails, we played in the sand and captured tiny fish using our thready towels as nets and crumpled chips as bait. Sometimes, Bruce and I would fish on the far side of the lake for the very plentiful bluegill using cane poles and worms we had dug from the backyard at home and saved in coffee cans.

Once I was fishing there by myself when I was nine years old. My brothers were swimming and my parents were golfing. My little sister was staying the afternoon at The Kenyon, a brick apartment building in Owensboro where our grandmother lived. Dad had let me use some of his tackle that he kept in an old woven cane basket, including a float made from a porcupine quill. He liked the oddity of that float and had

had it for some time, so I was excited to be able to use it. And it was great. It was very sensitive, so any time even a small fish toyed with my bait, the bobber reacted and I pulled out fish after fish until, in no time, I had a stringer full, although at that tender age, I kept most of what I caught, even ones far too small to clean. Everything was going great. I was tickled. Of course, the time came when I swung the cane pole to extend the line out even farther into the lake in order to catch larger fish and looped the line around a branch far above my head. I could see the quill, hanging enticingly above in the bough. I panicked. Dad's favorite fishing tackle was up in the catalpa tree. I pulled and yanked until the line finally broke and the bobber stayed in the tree. I looked up and saw it swaying, teasing me. It was lost. I felt horrible. How could I lose Dad's favorite possession in the entire world? What sort of horrible son does such a thing? Okay, I may have attributed too much value to his bobber. I guess that's why, in a pique of despair, I dropped my fishing pole on the ground and walked away in total dismay. And I walked. I walked along the dam of the lake, then I walked up the narrow lane that was the entrance to the club. I reached the state route that we had taken to get to Rockport and turned the way I knew was heading home to Owensboro. A few cars passed by, but I walked on the grassy area beside the road, my mind still buried in a deep funk. I walked the few miles of the state route until the road intersected the US highway that led home and I turned and continued to walk, my thoughts perhaps less self-condemning and more self-pitying now. Afterall, I was truly very sorry. Didn't I deserve some credit for that? I walked the six miles along the edge of the hot, busy highway, cars whizzing past, until I reached the bridge over the Ohio River. Now my legs were tired. I walked along the narrow ledge of the bridge over the river. The river was green and brown, and the currents swirled below around the pylons of the bridge. I reached Third Street in Owensboro. About that time Pop's white Buick Special came screeching to halt next to me. He was just coming across the bridge himself, a look of terror and anger across his face.

"Get in!" Pop yelled at me as he reached across and opened the passenger door. I saw my fishing pole in the back seat, roughly disassembled, Dad's little basket and my metal tackle box on the floor. So he would know I had lost his precious treasure. He no doubt despised me for my carelessness. I climbed in, ready to be chastised for not being more responsible of something so wondrous. "Where the hell have you been?" Dad looked at me as if I were a space alien. I climbed in and shut the door, my head hanging in pitiable despair.

"What?"

"Where have you been? How did you get here?" A car behind us honked and Dad looked in the mirror, a little annoyed with this driver who simply wanted to continue his journey. Dad pulled across to Lewis Street and parked. "We have been looking everywhere for you. How did you get here? You've been gone for hours!"

"I walked," I mumbled.

"You walked?" Dad's eyebrows arched.

"Yes sir."

"You walked from Rockport to here? Why?"

"I lost your bobber." I began to blubber. "I was fishing and I was putting the line out and I swung the pole and the bobber got up in the tree and . . ."

I saw the look of disbelief on Dad's face. "You walked home because you lost a fishing float?"

"Yes sir." I snuffled.

"Jesus Christ." Pop looked out his window. It was about as close to religion as he ever got, I suppose. "Come on." He did a U-turn across the railroad tracks that ran down the middle of Lewis Street and headed back over the bridge.

"Where are we going?" I watched the familiar scene pass by.

"Well," Dad began, his voice exasperated. "There are boats criss-crossing all around the lake, looking for you." I tried to imagine why they would be looking for me there when I was clearly here. "The lifeguards from the beach are swimming around too, seeing if you . . ." Dad choked up. Then I began to understand. Dad or my stepmother had come looking for me and found everything lying on the ground and no sign of me. After searching everywhere, they began to fear the worst. I started to tear up again but Dad put his hand before my face in a stop motion. "No, you don't get to cry over this. You aren't the victim. You did this, all on your own."

"But your bobber. . ."

Dad shook his head. "I don't care about that stupid bobber." He looked over at me and I saw his face turn to relief and maybe a little consternation as we rolled up Highway 231, Dad shaking his head slowly. I slunk around all afternoon after we went home, my brothers being both glad I was okay and put off by their day of swimming having been totally disrupted. That night at dinner, as Pop placed the baked herbed chicken and rice on the table, he said his ever-the-same prayer to bless the food, but somehow, he seemed to slow down a little bit and emphasize, "...and ALL of our many blessings. . ." I started in on my canned peach salad.

My other memory of Rockport was in late August of that year when a carnival came to town and set up at the fairgrounds. I don't think it was an official county fair, just one of the several travelling carnival shows that made the rounds back in those days. But we kids caught a glimpse of the bright colors and swirling lights and begged to go so one afternoon after a day of swimming, we got to go. There was the tilt-a-whirl, a small Ferris wheel, a clunky roller coaster, and lots of games where one could attempt to win stuffed animals. Dad told us not to waste the few coins he gave us on the games so we headed for the rides and other attractions. The first one we went to was The House of Mirrors, which was about the size of a small travel trailer. It had a glass front and neon white, red, and blue lights all along the bottom, sides and top. I was excited to traipse through the enchanted land of mirrors. Glen and I paid our money and went in. I followed Glen for a few steps, but then he took a turn I didn't see and I was on my own. I tried to follow him but bumped immediately into a glass pane. I tried to go another way but found myself looking at several mirror images of myself. I turned around and ran into another clear pane. I tried feeling my way, but kept seeing a multitude of my own hands, reflected from reflections until I almost wasn't sure they were all mine. I was lost in a house of mirrors. Then I did the only intelligent thing I could do and panicked. I kept walking around, desperate to find my way out but the more anxious I grew, the less progress I seemed to make. I turned and bumped and turned again. Every few steps seemed to take me deeper into the morass. Then I realized there was an announcer, extolling the fun of the House of Mirrors by commenting in a heavy midwestern twang on how utterly lost the dumb kid was. Okay, he didn't say "dumb," but it was how I felt. Finally, my frustration boiled over into tears and I stopped trying, convinced I would never find my way. It would be a sad story for the ages: a nine-year-old boy was lost in a house of mirrors of a travelling carnival and never came out. There would be rumors about his demise, perhaps tales about how his spirit still bumped into the mirrors and panes of glass, trapped for all eternity in this torment straight from the pages of hell. I stopped, my arms at my side, and looked out at the crowd of people, multiplied by the mirrors, gawking at me, laughing and pointing. The announcer must have seen my utter defeat, sighed and twanged lowly, "Look down. Follow the blue line." It was so absurdly simple I felt even more foolish, and the applause that arose when I exited the torture chamber was no help for my battered spirit. Glen could not stop laughing. I sat huddled in the corner of the backseat of our stepmother's huge Bonneville the whole ride back to town while Glen recounted the story and everyone laughed, even me, eventually.

We still went to Longfellow Elementary, Glen and I. We walked to and from school each day, hiking the block and a half up to Frederica and turning north the five blocks or so to the school crossing at 17th Street. Once we grew accustomed to the walk, we would sometimes vary it, taking Allen Street part of the way or cutting through the alley and down 21st Street. Usually my brother and I walked together, but I had made friends with Dana, who lived a block east of us, and Jimmie, who lived two blocks south, so I found myself walking with them frequently as well. We wore raincoats in the rain and heavy coats in the snow, but we walked just about every day. Some children arrived by car, the parents pulling down Griffith Avenue and up Alderson Court before letting their kids out at the back of Longfellow and exiting by way of the long drive that emptied back onto Frederica Street by Liken's Drugs. There were only a few times we were taken to school, and my memory was it had more to do with needing to take projects to class than in deference to the weather. Longfellow Hill was a great site for sledding. I recall one snowy day when school was cancelled due to the weather and half the city showed up to sled down towards the fence that separated Longfellow from the ROTC building and marching grounds of the high school. The rumor was the superintendent of schools drove by and saw all the kids at school sledding when he had decided they wouldn't be able to make it to school. We rarely had snow days after that. I decided once, but only once, that the sidewalk that led down the long hill towards Frederica Street would be perfect for riding down on a skateboard. I was saved by my total inability to keep my balance on the thing. The board itself was flattened by a Chrysler lumbering along the four lanes of congested after-school traffic. My skinned knee and bruised attitude were quickly forgotten.

I recall some of my teachers' names there at Longfellow. There were Mrs. Jefferson and then Mrs. Harrel, in whose class I was when Kennedy was assassinated. The principal played the radio news of the event over the PA system and I remember feeling lost and afraid. It had never occurred to me that presidents could be so mortal. I had Mr. Watrous and later a young woman who fell for the park ranger who came to give us safety lessons. They married before the school year was out.

That first Christmas on 22nd Street was a special one. Dad did not generally lavish us with material things. He had grown up in the Great Depression and had a keen appreciation for the transitory nature of wealth. But at Christmas, Pop could be downright generous and with the addition of our stepmother's income, that year they went overboard. We four younger children tumbled out of bed that Christmas morning and made our way with bleary eyes to the living room where we had decorated the tree some weeks before. The room was positively filled with presents. It was the very image of The Spirit of Christmas Present from Dickens. The needle-shedding tree was hidden by the expanse of gifts. There were bicycles for each of us, including a tricycle and red wagon for our little sister. There were games and models to be put together. Large Tonka construction vehicles that would surely destroy whatever was left of our lawn were lined up under the tree along with sets of smaller, die-cast cars and trucks. My oldest brother Bruce got a slot car set. Glen got a record player. I received a large cardboard puppet house with all of the characters of Snow White and the Seven Dwarves as hand puppets. I also received a large metal folding box that, when opened, revealed row after row of chemicals, test tubes, holders and even a burner that used denatured alcohol so I could do experiments. I was agog at the chemistry set, and all of it. We each received a Timex watch in our stockings. It was an abundance we had never known before. When we had lived on The Sows Ear Farm, we had barely scraped by. Now, we were suddenly flush. I took my chemistry set back to the bedroom I shared with my brothers and immediately mixed some selenium, sulfur, iron oxide, and water and put it over the flame of my alcohol burner, the test tube carefully locked above the flame with marvelous tongs that held it securely in place while the room filled with the foulest smelling odor ever. The room positively reeked, the scent hanging low and seemingly clinging to everything in the room. I have no idea what I thought I was making. I don't think anything was in the set that might explode, thankfully, but stink, oh yeah. Funny thing is, when I decided afterwards to actually read the booklet, it warned against just such types of chemicals being heated. Instructions. Who knew? We had to open the entire house and even turn on the attic fan to remove the smell, and it was cold outside. So, my first experiment in smoke bomb building a wonderful success, we all went out to ride our new bikes. There were pieces of furniture that still had hints of the foul smell years later.

Dad's marriage to our first stepmother ended nearly as quickly as it began. She had her own demons and we had enough demons of our own for any family so one day she was just gone. I don't recall Pop saying anything to us, but we all knew it was coming, and my older sister and my grandmother had been alarmed about the marriage for some time, so no one was surprised when it was over. It did mean the country club was no longer an option, but Bruce and I found a new place to fish, Johnson's Lake, which was more pond than lake, that sat at a far corner of a country club on the south end of town. Sometimes Bruce road his new bicycle out the three and a half miles to the lake, but I was not allowed since the journey involved a number of intersections I would not be trusted to navigate. Mostly, Dad took us out in his LeSabre he had traded for, our tackle and cans of worms tucked into the trunk, which was the size of some entire cars nowadays. We had graduated to fiberglass fishing rods now and plastic bodied Zebco reels that were nearly indestructible. We caught loads of sunfish that, if we cleaned them, Pop would fry up in cornmeal, salt, pepper and paprika using a combination of vegetable shortening and previously saved bacon grease. They were delicious and I even ate the tails. One hot day at Johnson's Lake, a hail storm blew up, sending Bruce and me to hide in a tin-roofed maintenance building while hail stones raised an awful din on the roof. When the storm was over, we went back to fishing.

If we no longer had the country club to entertain us, we did now have a renewed friendship with a family in Glenville, Kentucky, who were cousins of my Dad's in a manner I never could quite decipher. But going out to Lucille and Adrian's meant playing in the huge cornfield outside their back door and dining on feasts the like we rarely saw. Lucille was a great country cook and the spread she put on the table was always overwhelming in its abundance. Fried chicken, roast beef, ham, cornbread, biscuits and freshly baked white bread. Corn, spinach, macaroni and cheese, green beans galore, squash, the immensity was jaw dropping. There were even multiple dessert offerings, of which we enjoyed a bit of each, please. I looked forward to those Sundays, especially since having gone back to a single income had reduced the opulence of our own meals. I also liked playing hide-and-seek. I would hide in the cornfield and the other children would always have to call allee-allee-outs-in-free for me. Until one time they didn't. They just left me out, hiding in the cornfield, while they went inside to eat. I suppose every great skill has its burdens to bear. My amazing skill at remaining unfound had made me somehow invisible. But when I allee-allee-outs-in-free'd myself, I found everyone enjoying another of Lucille's wondrous meals. They were very generous to us. During late summer and into the fall for many years after that, huge bags of fresh produce would appear on our doorstep during the afternoon, sharing of a plentiful harvest from Lucille and Adrian.

One afternoon when I was 11, I was ambling around in the backyard of our house on 22nd Street, waiting for Bruce and Glen to come home from Southern Junior High School where they now went, when a woman came walking slowly down the alley. It was unusual for adults to be in the alley, really, except for the trash pickup and the occasional bicyclist, but they were infrequent. Alleys were the boulevards of children's play. That this woman walked so slowly, carefully, made me curious. She wore a heavy dark coat and a scarf over her head. It was chilly, but not as cold as she was dressed for. I stopped throwing the tennis ball against the back of our house and approached her, but not too near. She gave me a benevolent smile, her eyes moist.

"Are you Bruce?" She blinked slowly.

"No, I'm Larry." I saw her eyes fill up with tears.

"Larry? No. Larry? Oh, how you have grown." She retreated back down the alley slowly. I stood there for a moment. Who could this woman be who mistook me for my brother six years my senior? I went inside and sat in the living room, thinking. Pop came home from work with my brothers in tow. He brought some groceries in and placed them on the kitchen counter. I went in to help put away groceries (he would roll the canned goods to me so I could put them in a lower cabinet) and worked over in my mind what had happened. Pop looked up at me and saw me pondering.

"What is it?" He placed a can of tomato paste on the floor and rolled it towards me and reached back into the brown paper sack.

I looked at my Dad. "I think I just saw Mother." I corralled the can and put it in the cabinet.

Pop put down a bag of cereal he was pulling out of the sack and looked at me. "Where?"

"In the alley." I placed the can of corn he had rolled over to me in the cupboard.

Pop looked at me, his mouth set in a narrow line. "Yeah, you might have. Your mother is in town." Pop paused a long moment. "Would you like to go see her?"

"Yes, sir. I would." We finished putting away the groceries and he took me in the car to a small apartment building on Frederica Street. I spent the afternoon visiting with my mother who had been gone long enough I scarcely recognized her when she walked down the alleyway. I visited with her several times over the next few weeks. She taught me how to play solitaire with some battered playing cards she had with her. She also taught me how to play chess and bought me a small portable chess set. She got me a beginner set of oil paints and a small canvas that she kept at her apartment, since she herself painted quite a lot, and we sometimes simply painted in the same space for an afternoon, me daubing with abandon as she painted studiously. I had the impression that my knowing Mother was in town was a kind of secret, but I'm not sure if I remember that or if I just found her reappearance so mysterious, I attributed it all to a kind of shadowy event at the time. At any rate, a few weeks later, she was gone again to places I knew not. Unhappily, it was a recurring story.

By the time we left 22nd Street, I had two more important encounters. First, in the fourth grade, I met a bright, funny boy named George who would be my friend until this day. I feel very fortunate for that meeting. Then, in the sixth grade, I had my first girlfriend, Jane Ann, a fun, pretty blonde-headed girl who sat next to me in class. I was smitten from the first. That she also liked me I found amazing and disarming. After school, I would walk with her to her home on 17th Street across from school and we would sit for hours on her front porch, talking and swinging on the porch swing. Then I traipsed down Daviess Street, moony-eyed and happy, to home before it got too late. She was the first girl I remember telling my secrets to, my fears and my hopes.

Pressure Cooker Pot Roast with Ginger Snap Gravy

Feeds 6
<u>Ingredients:</u>
3-4 lb beef bottom rump roast
½ tsp salt
½ tsp black pepper
1 tbsp vegetable oil
1 cup beef broth

1 medium onion, chopped roughly
2 stalks celery, sliced into 1-inch pieces
2 large carrots, sliced into 1" rounds
2 medium potatoes, peeled and quartered
1 tbsp Worcesterhire sauce
1 bay leaf
6 whole cloves
3 ginger snap cookies

Directions:
Trim fat from roast and season with salt and pepper. In a pressure cooker on the stove, or if you are using an electric one, set on sauté, heat oil over medium heat and brown meat on all sides. Add remaining ingredients except for ginger snaps, place lid on cooker, reduce heat (if on the stove) and cook under high pressure for an hour then do a quick release from the pressure.

Remove meat and vegetables from pan and keep warm. Discard bay leaf and cloves. Strain pan juices and, if necessary, add water to make 2 cups and pour into a blender. Crumble gingersnap cookies into liquid and process until thickened to make gravy. Return the gravy to the pan along with the meat and vegetables and any juices that collected on the platter. Heat through and serve.

Beef Heart Stew

Feeds 6-8
Ingredients:
1 beef heart, thoroughly cleaned and cubed
2-3 tbsp all-purpose flour
1 tbsp vegetable oil
Salt and pepper to taste

1 cup beef broth
1 tbsp Worcestershire sauce
1 large yellow onion, sliced thinly

Directions:

Dust heart cubes generously with flour and season with salt and pepper. Sauté in a pressure cooker in oil until browned on all sides. Add remaining ingredients and seal. Cook on high pressure for 1 hour. Do a quick release and serve over egg noodles.

Canned Fruit Salad

This was a staple for Pop. Whenever he made it, he let me drink the canning nectar.

Serves 3-4
Ingredients:
1 14-oz can peaches, apricots or sliced pineapple rings
Iceberg lettuce
Cottage cheese (optional)
Mayonnaise
Cheddar cheese (optional)
Paprika

Directions:

Open and drain the fruit. Place a single large leaf of lettuce on each plate and top with two pieces of the fruit, cavity sides up. Put a small dollop of cottage cheese atop the fruit. (Pop sometimes left this off.) Top with a dab of mayonnaise, a shaving of cheddar cheese, and a sprinkle of paprika.

Baked Herbed Chicken

Serves 6, the way my Dad cut up a chicken.

<u>Ingredients:</u>

1 chicken, cut into four leg pieces, two breasts and a back. Dad used fryers.

1-1 1/2 tbsn olive oil

Kosher salt

Coarse ground black pepper

Herbs de Provence

<u>Directions:</u>

Heat oven to 425. Rub chicken pieces with olive oil and arrange on a broiler pan. Season the chicken liberally with remaining ingredients. Dad used lots of herbs and was always heavy on the pepper. Place into the heated oven and cook for 18-22 minutes until the skin is crisp and the meat is cooked through. Remove from the oven and allow to rest for 5-10 minutes before serving.

Room to Grow

The first time we saw the house we moved to on Halifax Drive was during an open house held by the builder and realtor. The entire concept of the house was definitely a new idea. All the solid walls had been prebuilt out of aluminum clad around plywood and Styrofoam. The walls were bolted to steel post framing along with wall-sized sliding thermal glass doors. It was the very essence of modern in my eyes, in the contemporary-style architecture of the sixties and seventies. It stood alone on the block which was a flat expanse of hard clay and scrub grass without a single tree on the entire block. Long and low, the house had a prairie-style feel and Pop was immediately in love. It was much, much larger than our little bungalow on 22nd Street, maybe 2500 square feet. Compared to the little bungalow on 22nd Street, it was huge. It had a covered recessed porch area that was glass and white aluminum with a small concrete bench on one end. Double doors painted blue led to a small entrance vestibule and a central utility closeted area (which in retrospect seems an unusual spot for the water heater and air conditioner unit). Beyond that was an open living room where we sprawled in front of the television, kids on the floor usually, Dad on the couch. Bonanza, Mission Impossible, Candid Camera, and especially The Fugitive were our regulars. There was adjacent to it a large dining area where we had more formal dinners: Christmas, Thanksgiving and Easter. Past the dining area where a glass panel shielded diners from the front door was a huge kitchen and family room. The rest of the house was carpeted, but this room had large white and black tiles for the floor. To the left was the kitchen with fluorescent lights above a very large island where the sink, built-in blender-mixer center, and dishwasher were located. It was a cook's kitchen. Cabinets lined the front of the island, drawers the back side where the sink and dishwasher allowed. There were two walls of upper and lower cabinets. It had a gas range top which was Dad's choice. Down from the refrigerator was a double oven. The cabinets were shiny yellow. Recessed lighting abounded throughout. Dad loved cooking in this kitchen. I can smell the beef stroganoff even now.

As large as the kitchen was, it did not take up the largest part of the room. The family room area was to the right and Dad put in a long dining table for everyday meals, a separate seating area, and a drafting table. With all of that, the room was still not at all crowded. A door led to an absolutely huge garage. It was a two-door garage, so ostensibly a two-car garage, but the width of the doors and the extra space within the garage, it could have easily fit three or maybe even four of today's cars.

The living room was mostly glass walls around a large central space. It was where the television sat after we moved in, but it was so light in the room, daytime television watching was problematic at times. The ceiling to floor drapes were so gauzy, they did little to cut the light. From the living area stretched a long hallway from which three bedrooms branched off to the left and a bathroom and the master bedroom to the right. The master had its own en suite bathroom. Every room had sliding glass doors from floor to drop ceiling. Most of the interior walls were white, the paint baked on at the factory. A couple of the bedrooms had built in drawers with walnut fronts. A few walls were wood-grained and a couple were green. Still other exterior walls were glass without sliding open. Central air conditioning, a dishwasher, modern built-in kitchen appliances, two bathrooms, a garage: these were all new extravagances to us. Dad had inherited some stocks and bonds years earlier from a wealthy aunt and now decided it was time to use those resources for what was pretty much his dream home. People often asked if he designed the house, and it was unusual enough to be custom, but he always said no, although there were many aspects of it he would have done the same.

Twenty-second Street was very residential. This new neighborhood was more transitional. We were at the edge of a subdivision, but we were also half a block from a convenience store and a fast food joint called Burger Chef, which had a big sign advertising 15 cent hamburgers. Another block north was a drive-in restaurant complete with car hops. Across the field behind our house looking south was the headquarters of Texas Gas Transmission Corporation, a national company that had set up its central operation in Owensboro in a beautiful steel and black glass international style building. It had an open courtyard area with fabulous acoustics. Once we moved in the summer of 1965, I frequently rode my bicycle over by myself to sing in that courtyard on the weekends when the place was empty. My repertoire was perhaps limited, but I do recall the mournful strains of "Last Kiss" echoing magically off the glass around me.

Another big change was my brother Glen deciding he would rather use his first name, Ernest, because Pop had told him he was the fourth Ernest Weill. Ernie liked that and liked the tradition so decided to be known by his first name rather than his middle name. It was a bit of a transition for me, but now, it seems he was always more Ernie than Glen. There were a few friends of his who called him "Ernie Glen" for many years, which I think at first was getting accustomed to the new moniker, but later I think was more a testament to how old their friendship traced.

Bruce attended Owensboro High, Pop dropping him off some days, although he bicycled the mile and a half most days. Ernie and I usually walked the three-quarters of a mile or so to Southern Junior High that stood on the corner of South Griffith and Booth Avenues, but Pop would drive us to school in his giant Buick Electra 225 if the weather was inclement. That Buick was huge. The car had fins, fender guards, automatic light dimming, and even a spotlight. The car was over 18 feet long. It was a true classic. Pop took Rhoda to Newton Parrish Elementary. She walked home each day. Returning home from school for each of us was pretty much on our own since Dad worked all day. This often meant instead of going home, Ernie and I walked to Wesleyan Park Plaza to hang out at Cibo's Pizza with our friends Sometimes we would wander down to traipse through Value Village a few doors down, although using the restroom there required having a dime for the door.

Since the format of classes at junior high school now involved changing classrooms and teachers for each subject, I met lots of new friends, although Dana and Jimmie were still prominent. I shared a locker with my good friend from grade school George. That's not to say we didn't have trials at twelve years old. George and I once got into a ferocious fight over his coat being dropped in the locker and, in retaliation, mine being dragged through the very dirty hallways of Southern Junior High and tossed into lost and found. I chased George down and caught him at Mayfair Square, and then we had a brouhaha for the ages. Busted lips, black eyes, broken bones, bruises and lacerations: none of that happened. Rather, we stood a safe distance from each other and cussed inarticulately, daring and dreading fisticuffs. I believe one punch was thrown and landed by each of us and that was pretty much our threshold. Okay, neither of us was exactly a ruffian.

Because we shared a locker, we had access to each other's textbooks. I once took George's spelling book home by mistake, and, always the wordsmith, filled in the crossword puzzle that was supposed to be done using the list of words for the lesson using vulgarities instead. It was quite the masterful achievement, getting the letters to match up in the proper spots. George was impressed when he saw it. Unfortunately, George accidently left his book in the classroom later that week. Ms LeMaster checked to see who had lost his book and found my handiwork along the way.

"George?" Ms LeMaster tapped her toe.

"Yes'm?"

"Is this your spelling book?" She glowered at the rapscallion. (That might have been one of the words we were supposed to learn.).

George swallowed hard. "Yes ma'am?"

"Did you fill in this crossword, George?" One eye-brow rose in heavy suspicion. If no one else knew the transgression, I certainly did.

"No?" George's eyes bugged out. I buried my head in my arms at my desk. George would tell. He would have to tell. I would be in such huge trouble. It had been a short but glorious ride into the seventh grade at Southern Junior High. Who knew what they did to miscreants who wrote vulgarities in spelling books? Reform school? Perhaps a beating at the hands of the vice-principal who seemed to relish giving "licks" with a wooden paddle.

"Then who did, George?" Ms LeMaster was having none of it. I was doomed.

"I can't tell you." George squeaked. I sat up straighter now. I couldn't believe my ears. George was not going to rat me out. What a great friend!

"I'm sorry?" Now both of her eyebrows were arched.

"No, Ma'am. I can't tell you." George looked at the floor now.

Ms LeMaster walked back to her desk and tossed the book atop her blotter. "You won't tell me. Very well. See me after school." A hush fell over the classroom as we all contemplated what horrors of punishment awaited George. My admiration for his resistance grew. He was heroic. What a guy! George's hand went up. Ms LeMaster gave him a baleful stare. "Yes, George?"

"Can I speak with Larry?"

Oh no. The gig was up. He hadn't told, but under the browbeating of the teacher, he had let it slip. Now, we were both destined for the salt mines.

"No. But both of you come see me after school." She smirked. I promise you she smirked, her devious methods having broken George. Oh, the subterfuge she had employed!

George and I had plenty of time the rest of the day to discuss what fate awaited us. No doubt, the punishment was severe for such horrible deeds, my defacing school textbooks with vile vulgarities and George refusing to tell on me. Beatings, expulsions, humiliations: what tools did junior high school have that we had never tested? Probably our fathers would be brought into it. Then what? Thrashings and banishments and tortures unimaginable were part of our expected mistreatments, although in fact neither of our fathers were given to harsh punishments. George and I talked about how awful it would be and the more we discussed it, the worse our imaginations made it.

Perhaps we should hop a freight and escape before they could abuse us so. That was a plan. We could hop on a slow-moving train at Frederica Street and 11st Street and head south, or wherever the train went since we had no clue the destination of the freight that ran through there. We actually discussed hopping a freight. Instead, we slunk into Ms LeMaster's classroom after school.

"Larry, did you write these awful words in George's book?" She stayed seated at her desk, immoveable, stern.

"Yes, Ma'am." I hung my head in both shame and dread.

"Erase them." She handed me the book and a large rubber eraser. I sat at the first desk and rubbed off the masterpiece of obscenities. George sat next to me and watched. It was a good eraser. The words disappeared. I handed the book back to the teacher, she looked it over and handed the book over to George. "Don't do that anymore," she said to me, then went back to her grading. That was it. George and I looked quickly at each other then stepped lightly out the door and took of down the hallway, the prospects of adulthood eventually arriving now assured. That evening as I sat down to Dad's broiled sirloin steak dinner, I wondered what the hobos on the L&N boxcars might be eating.

Soon thereafter, the spelling book debacle was forgotten when the Beatles came to my little hometown of Owensboro and stayed at the modern high-rise hotel, Gabe's Tower. Gabe's Tower was the brainchild of a local businessman, Gabe Fiorella, who had started out with a restaurant downtown long before I was around. He moved out to 18th and Triplett Street where Gabe's Restaurant became one of the top fine dining spots in the area for many years. Mr. Fiorella expanded his dream, building a shopping center adjacent to the restaurant, then Gabe's Tower on the same block. At thirteen stories, it was the tallest building in Kentucky west of Louisville. It was a round building made of glass and aluminum and had a pool on the all-glass top floor. It was quite the upscale spot in Owensboro. We kids thought it was impressive enough to sneak into and swim in, but cool enough for the Beatles?

It was a Saturday and Dana called me early. "You have to come!"

"What? I was still asleep."

"Well, wake up! The Beatles are here." Dana screamed over the phone. We were both early devotees of the Beatles. We had Beatle haircuts, which barbers seemed to loathe. We knew the words to every song and which of the lads had written them. We knew the b-side of every a-side. We were heavy into Beatlemania. But here? In Owensboro? It's true, they had recently toured America. Could this be true?

I was skeptical. "Dana, why would the Beatles be here?" I rubbed sleep from my eyes.

"I don't know, but you'd better get here. I'm going over to Gabe's Tower. That's where they are." He hung up. I didn't debate myself long. If there was any possibility whatsoever, I had to see. I dressed in my white Levi's and bleeding madras shirt and put on my Bass Weejuns. I was young, but I knew if The Beatles were at Gabe's Tower, so would be every teenaged girl in town. I went in to the kitchen to tell Pop where I was going. He was just serving up some sautéed mushrooms on English muffins for breakfast. I sat for a quick bite. On school days, breakfast was usually cereal, either cold from a huge bag or hot oats or cream of wheat. But on the weekend, Pop liked to cook so today it was mushrooms and English muffins. I sat at my usual spot, my back to the bifold doors that opened to a pantry.

Dad scraped mushrooms onto my toasted muffins. The buttery, earthy smell enticed me. I was ready to dig in, but my siblings had to come to breakfast. I sat impatiently. What if Ringo checked out of the motel before I got there? Maybe even now, John was swimming in the pool on the top floor. "Where are you off to?" Dad looked me up and down, still holding the skillet with a hot pad, a spoon gripped in his other hand. "Aren't those school clothes?" He paused at the shirt. He never quite understood why one would purchase a shirt you knew was going to bleed out at every washing.

"Going to see The Beatles!" I beamed with excitement.

Pop's eyebrows rose. "Really." He turned and put the skillet on the stove and went to the cabinet for another plate. I thought he was astonishingly placid for such momentous news. Ernie came into the room in time to hear me explain what little I knew from my phone call. He shook his head in disbelief and we started eating as Rhoda and Bruce came in.

I pedaled on my stingray bike as fast as I could to Dana's house on Booth Avenue and together, we biked over to Gabe's Tower. It was a mile to Dana's house, then another mile to the motel, so by the time we arrived, my skinny legs were worn a bit, but once we arrived, I forgot about all that. There were hundreds and hundreds of teens all over the place. They were everywhere. They stood around on 20th street, blocking cars until the drivers gave a honk to wake them out of teenaged daze. They stood in small groups on Sweeny Street, blocking the entrance to W. T. Grants and the drug store beyond. A group of boys my age, although I didn't know them, were horsing around right in the covered portico of the motel. All of the boys had Beatle haircuts. I was astounded by the sheer numbers. Some girls giggled near me and I realized there was a car right behind me while I stood agog in the middle of the street. The car honked again and I straddle-walked the bike out of the way. I was incredulous. There, on the marquee, was the evidence: Welcome John Paul George and Ringo. So it was true! The Beatles were spending the night in my hometown. Dana and I hung around for hours. Some kids left but new ones arrived to take up the vigil. We had only to wait until some amazing long limousine arrived and we would capture a glimpse of the Fab Four. We rode our bikes around in circles and chatted with some girls, whom we impressed greatly with our knowledge of The Lads. As we grew restive, we ventured into the shopping center itself and rode up and down the sidewalk on Triplett Street. Police cars patrolled slowly through the area. Finally, a man came out and everyone crowded around as he announced sonorously, "The Beatles are not here. It was a joke. Sorry. Go home."

The disappointment was palpable in the crowd of teens. No Beatles. Yes, after an entire Saturday spent waiting and watching, even the most ardent believers among us (That would be Dana.) had grown increasingly suspicious that this was just some mistake, a prank. We all stood there numbly for a bit, then started straggling away to our homes, disappointed and tired. I biked the two miles home, went into my room I shared with Ernie, and listened to Beatles 65, both sides, several times. I allowed myself to imagine walking up to Sir Paul and shaking his hand one day.

As disappointing as it was, the talk of the Beatle-mania event took over the school for the next few days, but since teenage attention spans are notoriously short, we moved on. We were inventive brats back then, being particularly tough on substitute teachers. For one teacher, when she turned her back, two entire rows of pupils switched seats so that when she turned around, we were not where we had been. She did a double take then a triple take, doubting her own sanity. When one interim called roll, we told her odd, inaccurate pronunciations of our names, which she then called us the remainder of the day. We wrote mocking statements on the chalk boards while the teacher was in the hallway. Perhaps the most insidious trick was when our new friend Sam whispered to the substitute teacher to ask George why his sister didn't take dance lessons. She demurred at first but then said, "George?"

"Yes?" George raised his hand innocently.

"Why doesn't your sister take dance lessons?"

George's jaw dropped in disbelief. His face filled with agony. "How could you?" He whispered just loud enough for everyone to hear.

"What?" The teacher fumbled with some papers.

"I can't believe you asked me that." George looked at the poor substitute with mock scorn. "Everyone knows my sister has no legs."

The teacher stood motionless, her face started glowing red, and she searched her mind for the right words to say until the class erupted into laughter, having heard this ruse play out before with other unsuspecting substitutes. We were equal opportunity abusers. The fulltime reading teacher, Mrs. Glenn, was a distant relative of our family, again in ways I never completed sorted out. She had taught reading at Southern Junior High for many, many years. She particularly loved the Rudyard Kipling story "Rikki-Tikki-Tavi" in which a mongoose bravely saves a family. It was in her lesson plan every year. She was famous for it. The lesson she wanted us to take from the story was "perseverance," although even at the time, I thought it was more about courage and loyalty. Nonetheless, as she read the story to us in her quaky voice, we grew impatient and began making up excuses to go to the front of the class, to sharpen our pencils and the like. While behind the teacher, we would feign slapping her head, smacking instead our legs so it would appear as if we had actually slapped Mrs. Glenn at the same time Rikki the mongoose battled Rag the cobra. Mrs. Glenn simply read on, oblivious. I suspect the lesson was lost on the giggling students, but she read on.

I never told Dad about our torturing his second cousin once removed, but I suspect he would have disapproved of our motives but liked our creativity. Pop was very creative and moving into the house on Halifax Drive brought him out. He had a new energy, borne from how much he liked the house, as well as the fact he had the room to do so. First off, he bought some new furniture. There were metal bunkbeds and single beds for each of us kids. They were somewhat industrial-looking and I think had something to do with a dormitory he was designing, but I don't know more than that. He bought a long, sleek Scandinavian-style couch for the living room and a single pedestal dining table, all white polypropylene and oval. He purchased two leather and steel swiveling sling chairs for his drafting area in the family room. But more than the new purchases, Dad made furniture for his new house. He liked to make tables from raw interior hollow core doors which he stained and painted the edges black. In this way, he made tables for the whole house. He attached screw on legs and made a dining table from a hollow core door for the family room. He designed a short, long steel frame that he had welded together from one-inch square steel tubing and made a low table for the television and a splay of Life magazines. He made a table for the telephone area, this one held up with small gold chains from the wall above. He also made a small framed plant holder of a wooden frame with cardboard nailed to the underside, filled it with a single later of river gravel, and put a round-bottom

Lucite pot with bamboo sticking out for the corner of the living room. He made his own swag lamps using paper lanterns. He even made his own drafting table.

His creativity also grew in his cooking. He had always been a fan of tomato aspic so he started making his own. He made sauerbraten and braised short ribs in the pressure cooker. Although he was not generally a baker, he was intrigued by Boston brown bread baked in a coffee can so he made that. Having a full kitchen with lots of room and the appliances he wanted, he spoiled us with all of these delicious foods. The move to Halifax Drive expanded all of our worlds. Moving to Halifax Drive seemed to redefine who we were, both as a family and individually. It was an important inflection point in our family history.

Beef Stroganoff

Serves 6
Ingredients:
2 Pounds ground beef
Salt and pepper to taste
4 Tablespoons butter
1 Pound sliced mushrooms
1 Large white onion, sliced
2 Cloves garlic, minced
1/4 Cup all-purpose flour
3 Cups beef broth
1 Tablespoon Worcestershire sauce
2 Teaspoons Dijon mustard
1 Teaspoon paprika
½ teaspoon ground nutmeg
1/2 Cup sour cream

10 Ounces cooked egg noodles

Instructions:

In a large cast-iron skillet, brown the ground beef thoroughly. Season with emphasis on the black pepper. Remove the meat from the pan into a colander to drain and set aside.

Melt the butter in the same skillet.

Cook the mushrooms, onions, and garlic until tender.

Sprinkle the flour over the cooked vegetables in the skillet and stir for a minute.

Turn the heat to low and stir in the beef broth slowly.

Allow the broth mixture to come to a simmer and thicken.

Once the mixture has thickened, stir in the Worcestershire sauce, Dijon mustard, paprika, nutmeg, and sour cream.

Stir in the reserved beef and simmer over low heat for 5 minutes.

Serve over hot cooked egg noodles.

Broiled Sirloin with Black Pepper, Mushrooms, and Onions

Serves 3-4. Pop always fixed two steaks for dinner for our larger family.

Ingredients:

Extra-virgin olive oil

2 pound sirloin steak

Kosher salt

1-2 teaspoons ground black pepper

1 large yellow onion, cut into rings

½ pound white mushrooms, cleaned and sliced thickly

2 cloves garlic, minced

1 tablespoon butter

Dash Worcestershire
Salt and pepper

Directions:
Preheat oven to broil.

Brush steak with olive oil. Season both sides of steak generously with salt and pepper.

Place the steak on a broiler pan and broil for 3 ½ minutes. Flip it over and broil for another 3 ½ minutes.

While steak is cooking, place onions, mushrooms, garlic and butter in large skillet over medium high heat and cook until onions are translucent. Add a dash of Worcestershire sauce and season to taste.

Transfer steak to a plate to rest.

Pour any steak juices from the resting steak into the skillet of vegetables. Transfer the steak to a cutting board and slice into 1/4-inch slices. Lay the steak slices on a platter and pour vegetable mixture over top and serve with baked potatoes.

English Muffins with Mushrooms

Serves 4
Ingredients:
4 English muffins, halved by piercing with a fork all around, and toasted
1 pound white mushrooms, cleaned and sliced thinly
1 Tbsp butter
Salt and pepper

Directions:

Place the muffins on plates. Sautee the mushrooms in butter, season to taste and pour over the top of the mushrooms. Dad sometimes fixed scrambled eggs with this which he put on the English muffins before putting on the mushrooms.

Tomato Aspic

Combine 2 cups tomato juice, ¼ cup chopped onion, ¼ cup chopped celery, 2 tablespoons brown sugar, 1 teaspoon salt, 1 bay leaf, and 4 whole cloves in a heavy saucepan, cover and simmer for 5-7 minutes. Strain. Soften 2 tablespoons unflavored gelatin in 1 cup cold water. Stir in the hot juice mixture and add 1 cup cold tomato juice and 3 tablespoons lemon juice. Pour into 5-cup ring mold and chill until set. (Some people like to stir in chopped celery when it is partially set.) Unmold on a bed of lettuce.

Sauerbraten

Serves 10
Ingredients:
2 medium yellow onions, sliced
½ lemon, sliced
2 ½ cups water
1 ½ cups red wine vinegar
12 whole cloves
6 bay leaves
6 whole black peppercorns
1 tablespoon brown sugar
1 tablespoon kosher salt

¼ teaspoon ground ginger
4-pound beef rump roast
Vegetable oil
Ginger snaps

Directions:
Combine all ingredients except oil and ginger snaps in a large bowl, cover and let sit in refrigerator for 36 hours. Remove roast and pat dry and strain marinade. Brown the roast on all sides in vegetable oil in a large Dutch oven. Add reserved marinade and cook slowly for at least 2 hours until very tender. Remove the meat. Add crumbled ginger snaps to the pan sauce and stir until thickened (about 1/3 cup cookies to each cup juice).

Pressure Cooker Braised Short Ribs

Serves 6
Still one of my favorites.
Ingredients:
6 large beef short ribs
Salt and pepper
2 tablespoons vegetable oil
3 slices bacon, finely chopped
1 large onion finely chopped
4 garlic cloves, minced
¾ cup dry red table wine
1 cup carrots, cut into 1 ½" sections
1 can beef consommé
3 tablespoons tomato paste
1 tablespoon flour
1 tablespoon butter

Instructions:

Season ribs generously with salt and pepper. Add oil to the pressure cooker, select sauté. When the oil is hot, brown the ribs on all sides in small batches without crowding. As the ribs brown, remove them to a plate.

Add bacon to pressure cooker and keep it on sauté. Cook until brown and crisp. Spoon out all but 2 tablespoons of the bacon fat. Add onion and sauté until translucent, about 3 minutes. Add garlic and cook one minute.

Add wine and with a wooden spoon, scrape up any brown bits stuck on the bottom of the pot. Add carrots, consommé, tomato paste, and ribs to pressure cooker, cover and lock lid. Under High Pressure, cook for 40 minutes. Do a natural pressure release for 10 minutes and then release any remaining pressure.

Remove ribs to a platter and cover with foil to keep warm.

Knead together the flour and butter into a ball. Add to the liquid in the pot, turn the pot to sauté, and bring to a boil, stirring constantly until sauce thickens. Turn pressure cooker off.

Add ribs and stir to coat. Return the lid to the cooker and let the ribs absorb the sauce for about 10 minutes, stirring occasionally.

Serve over noodles.

Boston Brown Bread

Ingredients:
Butter
1/2 cup all-purpose flour
1/2 cup pumpernickel rye flour
1/2 cup finely ground corn meal

1/2 teaspoon baking powder

1/2 teaspoon baking soda

1/2 teaspoon salt

1/2 teaspoon ground allspice

1/2 cup blackstrap molasses

1 scant cup buttermilk

1 teaspoon vanilla extract

1/2 cup raisins

One metal 6-inch tall by 4-inch diameter coffee can, thoroughly cleaned and dried

Instructions:

Preheat the oven to 325°F. Bring a large pot of water to a boil over high heat.

Grease the coffee can with butter.

In a large bowl, whisk together the dry ingredients: all-purpose flour, pumpernickel flour, corn meal, baking powder and soda, salt and allspice. Add the raisins.

In another bowl, mix together the buttermilk and vanilla extract if using. Blend in the molasses.

Pour the wet ingredients into the dry and stir well with a spoon.

Pour the batter into the coffee can taking care that the batter not reach higher than 2/3 up the sides of the can. Cover the coffee can tightly with foil. Put the can in a high-sided roasting pan.

Pour the boiling water into the roasting pan until it reaches one third up the side of the coffee can. Put into the 325°F oven. Steam for 2 hours and 15 minutes. Check to see if the bread is done by inserting a toothpick into it. If the toothpick comes out clean, it is done. If not, re-cover the pan and cook further checking every 15 minutes.

Remove from the oven and let cool for 10 minutes before putting the coffee can on a rack. Let the bread cool for 1 hour before turning out of the can. Great with cream cheese.

En Passant

JG loves LW. That's what it said. I saw it scribbled all over her blue canvas, three-ring notebook, a rainbow of declarations in pencils and pens, sometimes bold block letters, sometimes fluffy over-lapping rounded letters. Some places, it was within large hearts, other times only surrounded by hearts and occasional flowers (daisies, I believe). I stood there minding my own business, letting "Walk Away Renee" flow through my head, having heard it earlier, when I glanced over, and there was a notebook covered with my initials. I wondered if LW was me, Larry Weill. Of course, since I didn't know the girl, I doubted it; but it was possible. It could be Lonnie Walker, but who would like him? He was short and buck-toothed. Or maybe Lance Whitaker. He was popular, but he had "liked" Sandy Harper since the sixth grade. Or, it could be me, and while I too had a girlfriend of sorts, Leslie, we weren't going together, exactly. She didn't have my ID bracelet anyway.

Besides, this girl was cute, for a seventh grader. I mean, as an eighth grader, I ran in a much faster crowd than she possibly could as a seventh grader. And I didn't know she was a year younger, but I figured she was since she was standing with that group of kids watching our football team, the Southern Junior High Rebels, going down to their fifth loss in five tries. We were nothing if not consistent. But what did we care? It was something to do on a wonderfully clear, brisk fall afternoon and everyone was there, and besides, the Sno-Cone truck would be by selling bubblegum flavored cones for fifteen cents apiece, a mound of ice and a squirt of sickly sweet syrup that would turn your mouth and anything else it touched a nice pale blue. I didn't know her name, though – who was JG? Jane? Jessica? Jackie? She stood next to me, as if she was with me, advertising that she loved someone with my initials. I had to ask. I fidgeted a little, wiped a bit of smudge off one shoe with the other, adding to the size of original smudge. I locked my hands behind me and swung back and forth, an awkward motion I tried to give up but for some reason found self-perpetuating. Finally, I unlocked my fingers, pulled my arms around and cleared my throat.

"Um, who is LW?" I said to her shoulder, since she was a good four inches taller than me. She turned and looked at me, her face a mixture of surprise, fear, and bewilderment. She glanced down at her notebook, held against her chest with both arms crossed in front, then back at me, her face contorted now in what could only be described as horror. She let out a small, "Oh!" then turned and ran away, crying. I watched her run behind the metal bleachers and disappear behind a gaggle of legs. I looked over to the kids she had been standing with and shrugged. In return, I received a collection of frowns and head shakes. What had I done? All I did was ask her who LW was. I shuffled over to the group, three girls and a sickly looking boy with thick glasses and a protruding mouth of gleaming metal braces. They probably wanted to walk away, but being a year older gave me some staying power.

"What was that about?" I jerked my thumb in the general direction of the girl's retreat.

"I'm so sure you don't know," one red-headed girl with a face of freckles sneered.

"What?" I shrugged again. She eyed me closely.

"You don't know?"

"Know what?"

"Janet likes you." She said "likes" that special way that says she had a crush on me. Janet, huh?

"Janet likes me?" I felt quite flattered. The red-head nodded. I felt warm inside. It's nice to be loved, even by a seventh grader. I looked over to the bleacher. "What's Janet's last name?"

"Gish." The red-head was my confidante now. "Janet Gish. She's actually been in love with you a long time." She leaned closer to me, so the details wouldn't be public to just everyone. It wasn't lost on me that we had gone from like to love in fifteen seconds.

"Yeah? How long?" I found myself whispering.

"About a month and a half. Ever since you held the door open for her at the tardy bell that day." I tried to picture it, but couldn't. It's true I held the door open for the others. As a patrol boy before school, it was part of my duties.

That was it, no doubt. They always fall for the uniform. Well, I didn't actually have a uniform, just a white strap that went around my waist and across my body over my shoulder, with a genuine silver-colored shield over my heart. But it was official, no doubt blinding to younger kids entrusted to my care as I stopped traffic with my red-flag-on-a-stick traffic stopper. I herded my little sheep across the side street with George on the other side stopping traffic from the other direction. It was glorious. We told these adults driving their Fords and Chevys to stop, and they always obeyed, mindful I'm sure of the badge on my chest. No doubt they otherwise would have mowed down these hapless children in our care. When the stream of children slowed to a trickle, the boys closer to school called us in by waving their red flags, and we waved our flags to call in the boys down the side street. They ran to our corner and we shepherded them across, then all four of us went to the big street and crossed with the two boys there. I was impressed by the planning that went into the process. I had my sights on the ultimate prize, though, putting up and taking down the flag. That required arriving earlier and knowing the proper flag etiquette, the folding and so forth, but I had studied it all and I knew, I just knew, I would rise to that esteemed level before the end of the year.

"Well, I didn't know." I looked over to where she had run off, but couldn't see her. I knew what I had to do. I walked around the cinder track that enclosed the football field where our poor, skinny quarterback Mac Griffin was being knocked flat by big Henry Kirkendahl, whom I remembered being nearly six feet tall and a hundred and seventy pounds in grade school. Mac might be that size when we hold our twenty-year reunion. I waved to Sam and George sitting in the bleachers with Joanne and Margot, the focus of all their attention not given over to Archie comics, stingray bicycles, firecrackers, Miss Fortson the young single math teacher, and French fries. At the far end of the bleachers, my once-secret admirer leaned against the rusty pipe supporting the seats above, wiping her cheek with her palm. Poor Janet Gish, whom I had never even noticed, was crying over me, but I didn't quite know why. All I had done was ask her who LW was. It really could have been Lance Whitaker, for all I knew. I ambled up beside her and just stood there for a moment, trying to figure out what to say. Finally, she noticed me and spun on her heels to face me. Her eyes were red and opened as wide as I could imagine them being open. She stared at me, nearly motionless, except, perhaps, for a slight tremble. I have heard that a baby rabbit's heart can burst with fear if you pick it up and hold it. I got the distinct impression a similar disaster was about to strike the bunny Janet if I didn't say something quick.

"Hi, Janet." I gave my best smile, the one generally saved for school pictures. Her eyes filled with water. I had to distract her. I turned and looked at the field where a squat runner from Eastern Junior High ran gleefully towards the goal, our skinny tacklers meekly throwing themselves towards him, either landing well short or crumpling if they actually ran into him. Another touchdown for Eastern. The scoreboard read 42-0, and the second half had barely begun. "So, think we'll stage a comeback?" I nodded towards the field. I was being so smooth – if only I had a moustache.

"Uh-huh." She shook her head slowly, still staring at me. I wondered what the first aid treatment was for a burst heart.

"I'll bet we couldn't beat Longfellow Elementary." I gave a knowing half-smile, my eyes partially closed in a movie-star look.

"No, maybe not." She blinked, her eyes less watery now. I was good.

"So," I turned and faced her again, "where do you live?" It was an odd question, I admit, but it's the only line an eighth grader really has.

"Um, Hill Street." She tucked her head a bit, timid and just a bit coy. I liked it. She held her notebook a little higher to shield her chin. She was pretty, with long dark hair and a dimple that I saw for the first time now as she gave me a faint smile. "Over near the park." Her eyes were much drier. "Where do you live?" There's just not a lot to talk about with a new girl when you're thirteen. I wouldn't discover that the problem only gets worse as you age until I was in college asking girls their majors and, ironically, where they were from, which is really the same question as where do you live.

"Over on Halifax, by Texas Gas." My body swayed a bit in the glow of her pretty smile. I glanced around me vaguely conscious I was seeing if Leslie was watching. Where did I go from here? I realized I didn't want her to leave. "Um, so, want a Sno-cone?" I felt a slight panic as I realized I wasn't at all certain I had any money, but then remembered I did in fact have a couple of quarters. I was flush.

"Okay." She brightened some more and seemed almost bouncy now. I realized that I was in a bit a whirl all of a sudden. My brain tried to grasp what was happening. Had I just gotten a new girlfriend, a girlfriend I hadn't even known ten minutes before? But such was our ease at the time. I didn't know, nor need to know, anything more than she was cute and she liked me, and, as any man will tell you, a girl who likes you is immediately prettier than a girl who does not. She walked with me over to where the panel truck with the faded painting of a purple Sno-cone sat at the curb. A short line of kids before us gave me the chance to take another look. She gave me that smile again and I felt something inside of me give a quick flip.

We walked back to the football field with our cones (she ordered cherry, a safe choice, giving her lips a bright red hue) and I let myself be seen standing next to her, right there in front of everyone. Leslie would know before I got home. But I didn't care. I had Janet who had declared her affections all over her notebook. The game finished, it was time to go home. Darkness would fall quickly this late in the fall. I saw George and Sam coming down the bleachers, alone, Margot and Joanne long gone, but my friends didn't seem to care.

"So, who's the girl?" George nodded towards Janet who was engaged in a serious discussion with the red-head and the sickly boy.

"Janet Gish." I looked at my pals and to my dismay, they began nudging each other, snickering.

"Larry's got a girl friend. Larry's got a girl friend." They sang in unison. The age old taunt. It never failed to be summoned, and, somehow, it never failed to goad a man.

"Yeah well, at least I'm not jerks like you two." It was weak, I'll admit, but it was all I could muster.

"Yeah, right." George stopped singing. He shook his head. "What homeroom is she in, anyway?" He said it scornfully. A man in junior high is on his own when he forsakes his friends for even a moment to give attention to a girl.

"I dunno." I shrugged. This would be difficult. "She's in seventh grade." I said it like it was a strong point, something to brag about. Maybe if I said it with bravado, George and Sam would be impressed. My hopes were quickly dashed.

"She's the same age as Sam's little sister, Larry. Ewwww!" George screwed up his nose.

"Gah, Larry." Sam was incredulous. "Why would you want a girlfriend in the seventh grade?" He shook his head in disbelief.

"She's not my girlfriend." I shrugged it off. "I just met her." Okay, I really did think she was my girlfriend, maybe. But denial provides its own refuge.

"Yeah, right," George said again. He was too close a friend not to see through me. "C'mon, Sam. Let's leave Larry to kiss his girlfriend good bye." He threw a wry grin my way as they walked away.

"I'm not gonna give . . ." I let it drop. They were gone, and, besides, I hadn't really thought about a kiss, but I wasn't against it in principle. I turned and looked at where Janet had been standing, but she was gone. Instead, the red-head was walking my way. I looked around and saw Janet almost to the edge of the school. If I ran, I could catch her. I started to make a dash for it, but her friend was right in front of me.

"Um, Larry." She wore a sympathetic smile. "Janet is dumping you." She nodded knowingly. I could only stare at her for a second and blink three or four times.

"Huh?" I finally managed.

"She's decided she likes Mac Griffin." My head spun. What just happened? Mac Griffin? Our quarterback who was now probably in traction? Mac? It made no sense. I didn't even know Janet a half hour before and now we had been boyfriend and girlfriend and broken up? I shook my head to stop the thoughts from spinning so haphazardly. "She still wants to be your friend, though." I was gawking now. Friends? The tired old I-still-want-to-be-friends routine? I couldn't stand it. By the next morning, George and Sam would be all over it, dumped by a seventh grader. My standing was severely damaged. I might never get a girlfriend again, and over what? A girl I didn't even know?

It was my first experience with the guiles of women. I was strictly a pawn in the social chess game of junior high school, and later high school, captured en passant. I walked home in a funk. I wasn't really upset over losing a girlfriend I never really had, and I was only a little worried about the abuse I would take from my buddies, my fall in the social fabric of junior high, or that I would also lose my unofficial girlfriend Leslie. But I was aware of my own vulnerability. I had been completely at Janet's mercy with only the shedding of a few tears, a blink of her eyes, and a dimpled smile. I had been a young, thirty minute fool for her, and the way I saw it, a young fool is as good as an old fool. Then, I decided I was mad. I didn't deserve to be treated so callously. It wasn't fair. That was it, I had had enough of women.

Dad came home from work and fixed a meat loaf and stewed tomatoes for dinner. He served up our plates and asked about our days, and instead of my more usual reply of, "Nuthin," I recounted my story of being liked and unliked within the course of one-half of a junior high school football game. My older brother Ernie snickered a bit but Dad raised a stop hand and he retreated to a steady smirk. Dad listened intently to my story. When I had finished, I realized my voice had become higher pitched as I got more agitated. Dad looked at me intently and said, "Give it time, son. You'll be okay." I thought I saw the beginning of a smile on his face too, but he suppressed it.

As I sat before the television that night with my family watching The Virginian, I vowed to never, ever allow myself to be treated that way again, to be a pawn in the game of love. Such was the depth of my foolishness, I believed it a vow I could keep.

Meat Loaf

Feeds 5-6
Dad often made stewed tomatoes in the oven when he made meat loaf.

Ingredients:
1 tablespoon olive oil
1 onion, chopped
1 green pepper, diced
1 stalk celery, diced
1 ½ pounds ground beef
1 teaspoon garlic powder
1 teaspoon paprika

1 teaspoon dried basil

salt and pepper to taste

1 tablespoon Worcestershire sauce

1 cup dried bread crumbs

1 egg

1 cup milk

2-3 dill pickle spears, chopped coarsely

1/3 cup ketchup

2 slices bacon

Directions:

Preheat oven to 350 degrees F.

Sauté the onions, green pepper and celery until the onions are just transparent. Put the cooked vegetables, beef, spices, Worcestershire and bread crumbs in a large bowl and mix with your hands until it is well mixed. Beat the egg with the milk in a separate bowl and add to the meat mixture, mixing well. Add the pickles and mix to distribute the pickles. Form the meat mixture into a loaf on a roasting dish. Pour the ketchup along the top and top with the bacon.

Bake at 350 degrees F for 1 hour.

Stewed Tomatoes

Serves 6

Ingredients:

1 (28 ounce) can whole peeled tomatoes, with liquid

3 slices stale bread, torn into pieces

2/3 cup white sugar

1/4 cup butter, melted

1 pinch salt

1 teaspoon black pepper

Directions:

Preheat an oven to 350 degrees F. Grease a 1 1/2 quart baking dish. Stir the tomatoes, bread, sugar, butter, salt, and pepper in a bowl; pour into the prepared dish. Bake until hot and the tomatoes are tender, about 45 minutes.

The People You Know

We settled in on Halifax Drive in a way we had not settled into a house previously. There was a permanence to this new home, probably resulting from owning it rather than renting, but also moving from a home that was older and perhaps more working class to one that was modern and upper middle class. It was in the suburbs but was also not like any other house in the area. Dad told me the builders had intended to build an entire subdivision using the technology used in building our house, but they had such difficulty selling the first one, they gave up that plan. That a developer owned the rest of the block probably explains why there were no other houses on that block ever built. In fact, the next buildings to be built along Halifax Drive on the south side were strip malls that eventually took over the entire side of the street (including the lot where our own home once stood). But when we lived there, the entire block was tall fescue, ragweed, and the occasional punctuation of a Queen Anne's Lace. Our own yard had been planted in Zoysia and it grew haltingly in the hard clay soil.

The soil was so difficult, I soon grew tired of wasted effort trying to garden and didn't take up gardening again until we moved several years later. But the Zoysia survived and grew well enough that in the full sunlight and warm weather, it needed mowing every week, which, of course, would be no problem with three teen-aged boys around to do that chore. That would be true except we were lazy and spoiled. Dad would remind us the lawn needed mowing. Then he would remind us again a couple of days later. Then he would bark at us a day or two after that. Then one hot summer afternoon, while three lazy boys watched "Where the Action Is," we heard the garage door open, which meant Dad was home. We watched television and waited for the door to open and Pop to come in, but instead, we heard the lawnmower start up and start chugging across the yard. We went to the front door and there was Dad, mowing the yard in his business suit, his face scowled. It was a hot day and even in our cutoffs, it was sweaty, and Dad began sweating through his clothes in no time. We ran out and took over the mowing, although at first he declined in a fury of frustration with us. He came in and showered, we took turns mowing and complaining how awful it was to have to mow in the heat and complaining how put-upon we were. Then we came in, cleaned up and ate the lasagna and tossed salad dinner Dad had fixed. He served up dinner as if nothing had happened.

I should explain that we always had dinner together during those days. Dad cooked away while we did homework or watched television. Then he would call us to dinner with either, "Come and get it or I'll throw it away." Or, "Does everyone have clean hands and a pure heart? Well, at least wash your hands." We all sat at the table, each in our usual spot, and Dad sat at the head, a stack of plates before him and the bowls and platters of food around him. Rhoda and I sat on his right-hand side, our backs towards the pantry. Dad's stepmother Chessie sat at the other end of the table from Pop when she was there. She was there often in the early years to watch Rhoda when she came home from school. Dad picked her up on his lunch break and took her home after dinner. She never learned to drive, drank the occasional beer, and smoked unfiltered Salem cigarettes. She reveled in taking Rhoda under her wing. Bruce and Ernie sat opposite Rhoda and me. At dinner, Pop would serve our portions, asking how much we wanted, then he would say grace (the same grace each meal) and we would dine. We put our napkins in our laps, we kept our elbows off the table, we did not talk with our mouths full, and we did not sing at the table. I never quite understood that last one. Before we left the table, we asked to be excused. If we had not cleaned our plates, we had explained to us that starving children in either India or China would love to have the food we were wasting. Somehow, the children hungry in our own town did not warrant a mention. Once Ernie asked why we didn't send the leftovers to India and help alleviate world hunger. His suggestion was not well received. He also wondered aloud if eating food we did not want was just as much a waste as leaving it. That led to a somewhat stony silence. Dad was, after all, a child of the Great Depression.

Pop was not much of one for leftovers so he tried to cook what would be eaten and not more. There was not usually much left on the plates of me and my brothers, but my younger sister Rhoda was a finical eater. Those days, she often did not like the strong flavors Pop cooked with and we boys would be long away from the table while Dad and Rhoda had a small battle of wills about eating. I can still see him drumming his fingers on the table while he waited for her to finish eating. Dad never considered cooking different plates for our differing tastes, but he did work into his routine some dishes he knew Rhoda liked, such as egg salad and shrimp with cocktail and remoulade sauces. We were spoiled silly with Dad's cooking and patience, although we tested the patience aspect often enough.

We discovered just how spoiled we were that fall when Dad agreed to help chaperone a camping trip with the boy scout troop since all three of us boys were in the same troop. We loaded up the giant Buick with supplies and headed up to German Ridge near Tell City in a caravan of scouts and fathers. Dad led the four of us to a flat area a few yards away from the rest of the troop. He had us clear away the brush and twigs and stones. We spread out a large tarpaulin then set up the tent atop that. He was matter-of-fact in his organization and I couldn't help but notice some of the other fathers following his lead on the process. We set up camp and then the scouts spread out and found firewood for a campfire. All was fine until suppertime, when the boy scout leader assigned one of the scouts dinner duty making a beef stew. Dad politely demurred, saying he had brought meals for himself and his sons thinking each family was providing for itself. The leader rather insisted, encouraging us to be a part of the whole troop. At first Dad agreed that it would be okay, but when he looked at the stew, he changed his mind.

What Pop saw was a large pot of greasy water from the ground beef being browned then water being dumped on top. Floating atop the grease were hundreds of sweat bees that had been attracted by the layer of fat on the soup. The stew itself was more discolored water and uncooked potatoes and carrots than anything else. Pop took us to our campsite and fixed grilled steak with sautéed peppers and onions with egg noodles on the side. The other campers, and their parents, were jealous. The next morning the rest of the troop had cold cereal. We had scrambled eggs and bacon. For lunch, the troop had peanut butter and jelly sandwiches. We had burgers with Dad's mustard potato salad. The troop leaders were not at all happy with him, but we were, and we realized completely how fortunate we were. I strongly believe the other scouts thought we were lucky as well.

Beyond the scouting, we made many new friends moving to our new house and attending new schools. At Southern Junior High School, I met a new friend in Sam who had an active sense of humor and a daring about pulling off jokes that was both astounding and hilarious. He and my friend from fourth grade George became very fast friends. There were also new friends in Rick and Mark as well, and Henry, Tate, and Bob. We hung around together and goofed off and acted silly in a way only thirteen-year-old boys can. One warm winter day after school, we decided to see just how many of us could successfully ride on the same bike at once to go to Cibo's Pizza for French fries and cokes. It turns out, fewer than six is the answer. I was the last one on Bob's bike, and although he was bigger than the rest of us, he could not manage to pedal with all the extra weight. We fell over. More accurately, everyone fell on me, since I was on the front. We were in a pile on the edge of Booth Avenue. My buddies were laughing and giggling, but I looked down and saw my leg bent at an angle it should not be able to bend.

"Let's try again," Bob said. He yanked the big Schwinn up and straddled the bar.

"Yeah," George chimed in. "This time I'll get on the back." George sat on the rear fender.

"My leg is broken." I kept staring at the Salvadore Dali portrait of my right leg.

"Oh yeah right, Larry. Come on, get up." Jimmie went to climb onto the handlebars. "Oh God, that's so gross!" Jimmie yelled. It wasn't a compound fracture, but my leg was twisted so unnaturally, it was startling. Leather-soled Weejuns have no traction on asphalt, evidently. We hadn't made it very far from school, so Jimmie ran back to get help. I think I was in a bit of shock, but I remember a circle of curious classmates gawking down at me, Mr. Casey the principal looking at me for about two seconds and leaving, then my Dad and the ambulance arriving at about the same time. Dad rode with me in the ambulance to the hospital, cursing at the inconsiderate drivers who did not give right-of-way to the ambulance. Broken femur.

My leg was put in traction for four or five weeks. I think it was that long. It felt like forever. I stayed in the hospital and watched television, which during the day bored me to no end. I read books, discovering James Bond and Dr. Fu-Manchu. I learned to hook a rug and spent a number of hours making a small seascape out of precut pieces of yarn. I had mystery riddle books and jokes books. Dad came to see me every day at lunch and usually brought me a snack. A tutor came by and worked with my studies so I wouldn't get behind, but I cannot really recall his being there often.

After my time in traction was served (yes, if felt a bit like a prison sentence to an active 13-year-old), I was affixed with a spica cast that went from my chest to my right toe. I spent the next six weeks lying in my bed that Pop had put in the living room, off to the side, so I could be a part of the family. I dined on a TV tray while the rest of the family ate in the dining room rather than the family room. In the evening, we watched television as a family, me in my bed, everyone else sprawled on the floor or on the couch. Dad put a very long cord on the phone so I could have use of it during the day. This was long before cordless phones. The tutor came by still, but again, my memory does not recall his doing much. Mainly, I read the antique edition of Encyclopedia Britannica that Dad had inherited from someone and I read in the Britannica Great Books collection he had bought more recently. I loved the encyclopedia. In the Great Books, I enjoyed The Odyssey and Jonathon Swift, but I took a real liking to Pascal's Pensées.

It was winter, so while Dana and Jimmie especially came to visit me on weekends sometimes, I had relatively few visitors. School was in session and the daylight was short-lived. Who could come by? It was lonely during the day. Dad brought Chessie out at lunchtime on some days to wait for Rhoda to come home, but she was engrossed in her "stories" most of the afternoon. Mainly, I read and fidgeted and felt sorry for myself. Then one day when I was alone, a knock came on the door. We didn't lock it since I couldn't get up to open it, so I yelled, "Come in!" In came three of my classmates, twin sisters Terri and Sherri and their cousin Peggy. Terri was ostensibly my girlfriend, although I had not had the opportunity to be around her much, of course. And Sherri had been my girlfriend prior to that. Such is the transitory nature of early teen romance. But I had not seen any of them in over a month. They had come to buoy my spirits, which they did immediately. I was very happy to have company. We visited for a few minutes. They caught me up on the latest news around the hallways of school, who liked whom and the like. They laughed at the jokes I had memorized from my jokebooks (how generous was that!). Then, they decided to play a game. They took a scarf and blindfolded me. With my eyes shielded, they took turns leaning over me and smooching with me. I was supposed to guess who I was kissing. It was a great game, in my opinion. I don't think I guessed right very often, and perhaps didn't try that hard because the more I missed, the more they tried to test my abilities. I was in a swoon by the time they left, giggling and waving. Yes, my spirits were definitely lifted. That night as the rest of family sat at the table and I leaned over my TV tray enjoying Dad's split pea soup, Dad kept asking me if I was alright. I suppose my smiling and staring off into space caused him to worry.

Being a teenager meant new friends as well as new challenges. Something that was quite new to me were all the various cliques in junior high school. I fit in pretty well, but I also had my self-doubts. I went to dances, but worried about being rejected. I tried out for school plays, but usually received small roles (probably due to a speech impediment I had then). I learned to dress in the popular clothes of the time and learned how to speak in the cool lingo. It was cool to dig a tuff fox and neato to go to a groovy movie with her, but a real drag if she put you down. I liked the dark paisley shirts with white cuffs and collars that some of the other kids had and finally got me one. I thought it was far out. But I was late to school the day I first wore it and received a "seventh period," which meant staying an extra hour doing homework while the assistant principal kept guard. He had a penchant for paddlings and, to my thinking, enjoyed the responsibility far more than he ought to have. I walked into the designated classroom and the warden smiled.

"Aren't you Little Weill?" Having older siblings created a certain notoriety, it seemed.

"Yes sir." I headed for a desk.

"Well, I'll tell you what, Little Weill. Old Faithful here," he twirled his long wooden paddle. "Old Faithful has a crack in her, and, well, I think she may only have one lick left in her. You take a lick, I'll let you out of seventh period. Whatta ya say?" He sneered at me. I didn't want to stay any longer, and besides, the paddle was cracked so it probably would break before it hurt much. And there was a football game in a few minutes, and I wanted everyone to get a look at my groovy new threads.

"Okay." I sauntered confidently to the front of the classroom and leaned over. Vice-principal de Sade reared back and gave my butt a very stiff whack. The paddle did not break, and I doubt seriously it had a crack. I think the Marquis simply used that line to trick unsuspecting teens. It smarted, and I mean a lot. But I managed to put on a smile, grab my books, and head to the door. By the time I reached the hallway, though, my eyes were watering from the pain. Ouch. A classmate, Teresa, walked towards me then. She was definitely in the cool crowd. She had no idea I had just gotten a wallop, but she saw me in obvious distress. She stopped before me, looked sincerely into my watery eyes, and said, "Well, Larry, it's okay. I LIKE your shirt." She gave me a kind smile and bounced down the hallway, pleased with her act of benevolence. I stood still for a moment, realized what just happened and burst out laughing. The vice-principal came to the doorway and glowered at me. I headed home.

They were simpler times in many ways. We youngsters travelled all over town, both with and without our parents' knowledge and consent. If we weren't always angels, we weren't usually demons either. We rode bikes over to the Babe Ruth park to watch baseball games on Saturday and talk with girls. Sometimes, we would remove the front wheel of one sting ray bike and affix the fork to the rear axle of a second one, thereby creating a tandem bike. It brought attention, but was awkward to ride since both riders could steer, sometimes at counter purposes. We rode our bikes to the shopping center, downtown, and across town to each other's houses. We would have sleepovers and sneak out to wander the streets by the bright lights of the street lamps in Owensboro, playing hide-and-seek with every car that drove by. Having sliding glass doors in every bedroom as our house did meant we were rarely kept in. If any girls were having sleepovers, we found our way there to hangout, although we never got beyond chatting up some girls who were leaning out the window to chat back with us. One thing we did we should not have was we would go swimming at a nearby swim club in the middle of the night. We learned the timing of the patrol car route. We watched for the police car to pass, then we would sneak over to the swim club, climb the chain link fence, swim around in the pool for twenty minutes, then return home before the next scheduled pass of the patrolman.

But we also stayed occupied at home. Especially in the summer, Dana would come over and we would invent games to play. Dana and my oldest brother Bruce got along well, and since Bruce was wiry but very strong, we had many a mock wrestling match with him. Pop always liked Dana and, because my father was the king of Dad Jokes, whenever he saw Dana, he would greet him with, "Hi, What's your name, Dana?" And Dana never failed to laugh. Once, we hid all of Rhoda's stuffed animals, and she had dozens of them. Then, she went on a safari with a toy gun. When she shot an animal with a "Keewwww!," we would push the animal over. She was delighted with the game. We turned the house into house of horrors once as well. Jimmie came over too. Sometimes, Jimmie and Dana were there at the same time, but I don't think they ran around together except when I was with them. Jimmie was very smart and had a wry sense of humor and a sense of daring. He was very skinny, so we decided one blustery day to make him into a kite. We tied a quilt to two long pieces of thick bamboo and tied the bamboo to Jimmie's ankles and wrists like da Vinci's Vitruvian Man. Then we tied a rope to Jimmie's waist and went out to fly Jimmie, who walked awkwardly across the field. It was windy enough to toss him to the ground several times, but never quite strong enough to actually fly him. Thank goodness. What if we had gotten him up twenty feet?

And Dad found a great way to make friends. He joined a support group for single parents. On the face of it, it was simply a way to have kindred adults who would understand the travails of raising children alone. But at that time especially, there were far more single mothers than single fathers. As a result, Dad was a bit like a kid with a dollar set free in a candy store. He was very popular immediately, being an available handsome man who had a nice car and a nice home and could cook. We went to picnics with the group a few times, Dad taking German potato salad or three bean salad, and the single mothers doted on us. Well, they were doting on him, but I didn't really understand that at first.

Despite being busy with us kids and his newfound dating trove, Pop knew other guys around town and sometimes devised a variety of get-rich-quick schemes with them. He designed buildings "on spec," hoping they would get funding or other needed approvals and he would get the job, which did happen a few times. He did the drawings for a local barbecue place that we all loved when the owner purchased the barber shop next door, receiving in payment sandwiches for the family for a number of months. We enjoyed that, but somehow the sandwiches soon got thinner and thinner until they were hardly more than buns with sauce smeared across them. He worked on a design for a chain of drive-in diners for a major soul singer whose manager was the son of a friend of Dad's. He showed me his schema: every restaurant would look like a giant 45 rpm record with the singer's name on the roof as if it were a record label. I thought it was very cool, but the deal did not go through. The most unusual scheme was when Pop bought at least a half dozen large, fiberglass individual saunas. They were brightly colored boxes the size of a small refrigerator with a fiberglass door. Water was poured into a hole at the bottom, then the "steamee" sat in the box, closed the door, and sweated out impurities. Dad had one in his bedroom, which we kids experimented with when he was not around. I found it unpleasantly warm. And we had a garage full of them that Dad was going to sell and make a small killing on. He never sold a one of them that I knew of until he finally got rid of them all at once. I suspect he took a bath with the steam baths.

We were happy on Halifax Drive, finding our footing and expanding our range of friends. When my wife Jennie and I drove back to see Dad years later after he had moved from that house, I often routed us past the house of Halifax, just to see it. Then one day, it was simply gone. I asked Pop what happened to it and he said it was still there. He and I drove over to the empty lot. It was gone. We asked at a small shop that had been built next door and they said the house was there one Friday and not there when they returned on Monday. We went back outside, and Pop looked at the empty for several minutes, then shook his head wistfully, and we went back to his house.

Lasagna

Serves 8 (But we rarely had leftovers in our family of 6)
Ingredients:
1 pound ground beef
3/4 pound Italian sausage
1 tablespoon olive oil
1 cup chopped white onion
1 cup sliced mushrooms
4 cans (6 ounces each) tomato paste
3 cups water
2 garlic cloves, minced
2 teaspoons sugar
½ teaspoon oregano
½ teaspoon dried basil
Dash of paprika

Dash of Worcestershire sauce

¼ teaspoon mustard powder

2 oz. red wine

1 teaspoon salt

½ teaspoon pepper

3 large eggs, beaten

3 cups small-curd cottage cheese

½ cup parsley

½ cup grated Parmesan cheese

9 lasagna noodles, cooked and drained

4 cups shredded part-skim mozzarella cheese

Directions:

In a large skillet over medium heat, cook and break apart the beef and Italian sausage until cooked through; drain in a large colander. While the meat drains, sauté the onions and mushrooms in the same skillet in the olive oil. Add the tomato paste (Dad opened one end, then opened the other end while holding the can over the pan.) and stir to mix the vegetables in and to get a slight cook on the paste. Add the next 11 ingredients and add back the meat. Bring to a boil over medium heat, stirring occasionally. Reduce heat; simmer, uncovered, 1 hour, stirring occasionally. Adjust seasoning.

Meanwhile, in a large bowl, combine eggs, parsley, cottage cheese, and Parmesan cheese.

Preheat oven to 375°. Spread 1 cup meat sauce in an ungreased 13x9-in. glass baking dish. Layer with three noodles, 2 cups cottage cheese mixture, 1 cup mozzarella, three noodles, 2 cups meat sauce, remaining cottage cheese mixture and 1 cup mozzarella. Top with remaining noodles, meat sauce and mozzarella. The dish will fill up so Dad often placed the baking dish on a cookie sheet with short sides to catch any overflow.

Cover with foil and bake for 45 minutes. Uncover; bake until heated through, 25 minutes. Let stand 15 minutes before cutting. Pop served it with a tossed green salad and crusty Italian bread.

Egg Salad Dinner

Serves 4-5
Ingredients:
8 large eggs, hard boiled, peeled and chopped
1/2 cup mayonnaise
1 teaspoon prepared yellow mustard
1 teaspoon lemon juice
2 tablespoons finely chopped onion
2 tablespoons finely diced celery
salt and pepper to taste
1/4 teaspoon paprika
4-5 Tomatoes, cut into eighths
Club crackers

Directions:
Place all ingredients except tomatoes and crackers in a bowl and mix thoroughly. Spoon over the tomatoes, add a dash of paprika for color and serve with crackers.

Shrimp with Cocktail and Remoulade Sauces

Serves 5
Ingredients and directions:
Shrimp:
1 lemon, halved
1 crab boil seasoning bag

1 teaspoon kosher salt

2 pounds peeled, deveined shrimp

Boil the lemon, seasoning bag and salt in a large pot of water for 5 minutes. Add the shrimp, cover and remove from heat. Let sit for 7 minutes, then drain and place shrimp in cold water to stop the cooking.

Cocktail sauce:

Combine in a medium sized bowl:

¾ cup tomato ketchup

2 tablespoons prepared horseradish

1 teaspoon lemon juice

3-4 dashes red hot sauce (to taste)

Remoulade sauce:

Combine in a medium sized bowl:

1 cup mayonnaise

¼ cup Dijon mustard

2 tablespoons lemon juice

2 teaspoons red hot sauce (to taste)

3 tablespoons olives, chopped

3 tablespoons sweet pickle relish

Kosher salt and freshly ground black pepper

Grilled Steak with Sautéed Peppers and Onions

Serves 4
Ingredients:
1 large sirloin steak, 25-30 ounces
Kosher salt
Black pepper
2 tablespoons olive oil
1 green bell pepper, sliced into strips
1 yellow bell pepper, sliced into strips
1 red bell pepper, sliced into strips
1 large white onion, sliced into thick rings
½ teaspoon garlic powder
Salt and pepper to taste (Dad was usually heavy on the black pepper)

Instructions:
Season the steak with Kosher salt and pepper and allow to warm to room temperature. Prepare grill over medium coals. On a separate burner, heat a large cast iron skillet over medium heat and sauté the vegetables in the olive oil. Grill the steak 4 minutes, turn and grill 4 minutes on the other side (medium rare). Let the steak rest a few minutes then carve in to individual portions and serve with the vegetables on top.

Dad's Grilled Hamburgers

Serves 4
<u>Ingredients:</u>
1 ½ pounds ground chuck
1 egg, beaten
¾ cup crumbled saltine crackers
2 tablespoons evaporated milk
2 tablespoons Worcestershire sauce
1/8 teaspoon cayenne pepper
¼ teaspoon garlic powder

<u>Directions:</u>
Prepare the grill on high heat. In a large bowl, mix the ground beef, egg, crumbled crackers, evaporated milk, Worcestershire sauce, cayenne pepper, and garlic using your hands. Form the mixture into 4 very flat hamburger patties. In the center of each patty, press your thumb into the meat to make the patty thinner in that area (This helps prevent the patty from shrinking into a ball.).

Oil the grill grate. Grill patties 5-6 minutes per side.

Mustard Potato Salad

Serves 6
<u>Ingredients:</u>
5 large russet potatoes, peeled and cut into 1 ½" cubes
3 eggs, hard boiled, peeled and chopped coarsely
1 cup chopped celery
1/2 cup chopped white onion
1/2 cup sweet pickle relish
1/4 teaspoon garlic salt
1/4 teaspoon celery salt
1 ½ tablespoon prepared mustard
ground black pepper to taste
1/4 cup mayonnaise
Paprika

<u>Directions:</u>
Bring a large pot of salted water to a boil. Add potatoes and cook until tender but still firm, about 15 minutes. Dad often boiled the eggs in the same pot. Drain and place into cold water to stop the cooking. Once cooled, drain thoroughly in a colander. Chop the eggs into large bites. Combine potatoes, eggs, celery and onions in a large bowl. Mix relish, garlic salt, celery salt, mustard, pepper and mayonnaise in a separate bowl. Pour sauce over potato mixture and turn thoroughly to coat all the ingredients. Sprinkle top with paprika and refrigerate until chilled.

Pressure cooker Split Pea Soup

Serves 6
<u>Ingredients:</u>
1 lb dry green split peas
1 tsp olive oil
2 large carrots, peeled and diced
1 medium onion, diced
1/4 cup diced celery
2 cloves garlic, minced
leftover ham bone
6 cups water
1 chicken bouillon cube
1 bay leaf
8 ounces diced ham
chopped white onion

<u>Directions:</u>
Rinse peas under cold water and set aside.

In a pressure cooker, add oil, onions, carrots, celery and garlic and sauté 4-5 minutes. Add ham bone, peas, water, chicken bouillon and bay leaf. Cover and cook on high pressure for 20 minutes. Let the pressure release naturally for ten minutes then release the pressure. Remove the bone and bay leaf add the diced ham and stir. Allow to thicken a few minutes. Garnish with fresh chopped onions and serve with crusty French bread.

German Potato Salad

Ingredients:
4 cups diced peeled potatoes
5 slices bacon
1 medium onion, diced
1/3 cup white vinegar
3 tablespoons water
4 tablespoons white sugar
1 ½ teaspoon kosher salt
¼ teaspoon ground black pepper
2 tablespoon chopped fresh parsley

Directions:
Place the potatoes into a heavy pot and fill with enough water to cover. Cover and bring to a boil, and cook for about 12 minutes testing for doneness with a fork. Drain, and set aside to cool.

Place the bacon in a large deep skillet over medium heat. Fry until browned and crisp, turning as needed. Remove from the pan and set aside.

Reduce heat to medium-low. Add onion to the bacon grease and cook until browned. Add the vinegar, water, sugar, salt and pepper to the pan. Raise the heat to medium high. Bring to a boil, then add the potatoes and parsley. Crumble in half of the bacon. Heat through, then transfer to a serving dish. Crumble the remaining bacon over the top. Serve warm.

Three-Bean Salad

Ingredients:
1 (15 ounce) can green beans, drained
1 (15 ounce can) pound wax beans, drained
1 (15 ounce) can kidney beans, drained and rinsed
1 small white onion, sliced into thin rings
3/4 cup white sugar
2/3 cup distilled white vinegar
1/3 cup vegetable oil
1/2 teaspoon salt
1/2 teaspoon ground black pepper
1/2 teaspoon celery seed

Directions:
Place beans and onion in a large bowl with a tight-fitting lid. Mix remaining ingredients thoroughly to dissolve the sugar. Add the sauce to the bean mixture, cover and let set in refrigerator for at least 12 hours.

All-ee All-ee Outs-in-Free

I was walking home late from Southern Junior High after watching our badly outmanned football team, the Southern Rebels, get trounced by Foust Junior High. The loss didn't bother me much, however, since I had managed to get the attention of a girl I liked in the aluminum bleachers at the game, although I am sure dripping the cherry Sno-Cone down the front of my bleeding Madras shirt was less than impressive. Still, I was happy and it was a cool autumn afternoon so I ambled lazily the ten blocks towards our home. The area was decidedly suburban, with long ranch houses on large lots. As I turned onto Monticello Drive, I saw the two teenaged boys leaning against the sign post. One was clearly older than the other and they were both older than I was at thirteen. I did not recognize them. They weren't from the neighborhood. They eyed me menacingly, the older one smoking a cigarette.

"Hey, kid." The older one waved towards me with his cigarette as I neared them. "C'mere a minute." I decided immediately going over there was a very bad idea, so I ignored him and quickened my pace a bit. Getting beat up on the way home from school seemed like a very unwise plan to me. Yet I had to walk right past them to get to my street. I sized up my options. Once I got past the corner, I would be able to cut across the field where houses were still under construction. It was still a long block to run, but I figured I had the advantage of knowing where the saw horses and piles of lumber were. I wished I had on my Chuck Taylors instead of my Bass Weejuns. "Hey, you! I'm talking to you, kid." I kept my face forward, but I cut my eyes so I could see them. He stood now from his casual lean and dropped his spent cigarette on the sidewalk and crushed it with his shoe, also a Weejun. I crossed to the other side of the street. I tried to look nonchalant, but I kept them in view. My knees felt a little wobbly. "Now why you suppose that kid won't talk to me, Bobby?" He glanced at the other teen, but he was looking at me, and clearly was saying it for me to hear.

"I dunno, Jimmy. Maybe he's deaf." I was almost directly across from them.

"Yeah? Maybe. Or maybe he thinks he's too good to talk to me." His voice gained a gravelly rasp I did not like. I tried to keep my gait at a walk, but I was definitely speed-walking at this point. I was almost abreast of where they were standing, the older boy with his arms cocked at his waist, the younger one looking first at me, then his cohort, then at me. "That it, kid? You too good to talk to us? Huh?" Jimmy yelled. He took off towards me, but at his first step, I was at a full gallop. Bobby and Jimmy chased me up the street and then behind the construction sites and across the field. Fear fueled my legs and I not only kept ahead of them, I eventually lost them as I made the corner of the half-finished house across the street from ours. I raced to our door, threw myself against it to open it, and jumped inside. Bent over at the knees, gasping for breath, I peered through the curtains to see if they had seen where I had escaped. I knew my younger sister would be already home, and my grandmother too, there to watch my sister until Dad came home. The two of them would probably be in my sister's room reading or playing a board game, but I also knew neither would be able to save me should Jimmy and Bobby catch me, whoever they were. I was doomed. There was no telling where my older brothers might be this late in the afternoon, and Dad would not be home for another hour at least. But the two boys who had chased me were not in sight in the street before our house. I felt a small wave of relief, but I worried about what might happen tomorrow or next week. Were they new guys in the neighborhood I would have to be afraid of from now on? Would they return on another day just to catch up with me, but next time jump me without warning? Scenarios raced through my young imagination. I left the window and went into the living room, where I could hear the television on. Both my big brothers were sitting there watching Boom Boom Cannon lip-syncing "Action" on American Band Stand. I felt much more secure then.

"What's with you?" My fifteen-year-old brother cast me a glance from his spot on the floor where he was watching the show. I realized I was still panting from my sprint. Our oldest brother who was eighteen looked back over the couch towards me, his expression only mildly curious.

"What's wrong?" But he turned back to watch the dancers doing The Pony.

"Two guys," I panted, "chased me." I spoke between gasps of air. "Home from . . . the corner."

My brothers turned towards me now. "What?"

""Two guys . . ."

"What guys?" My oldest brother was rising now. He had a sinewy strength that showed when he moved.

"I don't know." I shrugged.

"They from around here?" My other brother was on his feet now too. He was not much bigger than I was, but he was far more confident.

"No, I've never seen them before." I finally had my breath.

"They chased you home?" My two brothers came over to where I stood. "Are you okay?"

"Yeah, I got away." I looked from one to the other. Both of them wore deep scowls now.

"Where'd they chase you from?" My oldest brother was heading for the door and we followed. "They can't come into our neighborhood and chase you home." We caught up to him on the porch. "Where were they?" He turned to me and I saw his jaw clench. His anger was building.

"Over by Jackie's house." My two older brothers marched off, with me at their heels, up Halifax towards Monticello. Their reaction had been so immediate and strong, I wasn't sure what to think about what might happen if Bobby and Jimmy were still there. We turned the corner and there they stood, leaning against the same sign post, Jimmy smoking another cigarette. They saw us and I watched their bodies stiffen a bit, but they stayed at the corner. As we came up beside them, Jimmy dropped his cigarette and eyed us.

"What?" His eyes were half closed with a careful nonchalance. The three of us stood in a semi-circle around them.

"You chase my brother?" My oldest brother was fully flexed in every muscle. When he was very angry, he almost hopped up and down with fury, looking like some sort of government experiment gone terribly wrong. Every muscle twitched. It was a truly fearsome sight. His eyes were red with rage. My other brother, who had seen his share of fights, was far more deliberate. He sized up Bobby and I could see him ready to strike.

"Maybe." Jimmy spoke coolly while Bobby looked at the sidewalks and street to see where he might find an escape route.

"Why'd you chase him?"

"I dunno. Seemed like a good idea." He looked at Bobby as if it was a joke, but Bobby didn't respond.

"So, you wanted to beat him up?"

"He wouldn't answer me." Jimmy stood now with his feet apart, his hands in the back pockets of his jeans. My middle brother cut me a look as if to ask if it was true I wouldn't answer, and I simply shrugged. He returned his baleful stare at Bobby. My oldest brother was trembling with anger all through his arms and upper body, ready to pop.

"Well, we're here now. What do want to say now?"

"I forget." Jimmy was clearly getting nervous. He looked at my oldest brother. "All three of you gonna fight us?" But there was little doubt he would have no chance against my oldest brother without any need of assistance from puny little me.

"Both of you wanted to fight him," my oldest brother jerked his thumb in my direction.

"Yeah," Jimmy took a step backwards. "Yeah." He looked at the ground. "Bobby, maybe we oughta go home."

"Yeah," Bobby squeaked. They started backing up. I think my oldest brother was a little disappointed: all that adrenaline with no release. They turned and walked away.

"Don't come around here anymore. Stay away from our neighborhood."

"And leave our brother alone." We watched them saunter up Standish, turn the corner at Marycrest, then tear off down the street. I had always known having big brothers was a good thing, but I positively glowed with pride at that moment. My brothers had saved me from all those terrible scenarios that 20 minutes ago I had known would happen. My middle brother turned to me and smirked. "Try not to be such a dweeb." Both of them laughed and walked off towards home. I caught up with them quickly, just in case.

I spent what was left of the afternoon in my room, listening to Gerry and the Pacemakers and being glad. My grandmother hovered about, but we didn't say anything about the two boys at the corner. I picked up the book I was reading, A Wrinkle in Time, and lost myself in it. When Dad came home, I went out to greet him and give him a hug. He changed his clothes and poured himself a drink. He plopped down in one of his favorite leather sling chairs, smoking a cigarette, sipping his drink, and leafing through a Life magazine that had a beautiful woman on the cover. My siblings were squirreled away in their bedrooms. "Would love to go to Hawaii someday." Dad flipped through the pictures.

"Me too." I sat at the kitchen table. "What's for dinner, Dad?"

"Skloffmeadic on blanc with vistera sauce." It was Dad's customary answer that we understood to mean, "Wait and see, but it will be fancy." Then I spied the extra thick pork chops on the counter. That could only mean Dad's stuffed pork chops. My mouth watered. Dad loved to cook, but he had a fear of trichinosis borne from an earlier time so if he fixed plain pork chops, he tended to cook them until any trichenella left alive could not possibly burrow his way out, the chop was so tough. But when he stuffed them, the moisture made them stay tender and juicy. Dad saw me eyeing the chops and shot me a smile. He could always take the compliment of someone loving his cooking. "And corn pudding." He stood now to start cooking. I usually set the table, but otherwise I was occupied by sitting at the table, watching the maestro in action.

When we were all seated at the dinner table, Dad sat at the head, of course, the dinner plates and serving dishes in front of him. He said grace, a recitation that never changed, then dished out the portions. "Say when." He served his stepmother first, then the children in order of their age. When he had dished up his own, we began dinner. "Put your napkin in your lap," he reminded me. "What happened today?" Dad looked around the table. We told him about the two teens who chased me and the near fight afterwards. He listened intently. "You hurt?"

"No, sir."

"Good. If those boys come back, let me know, okay?" He was talking to my oldest brother, but the look he gave him was definitely approving.

"Yes, sir."

After dinner, Dad and his stepmother cleaned up the kitchen and he took her to her home while we theoretically did our homework, but I went back to find out what was happening to Meg Murry. When he returned, we all sat in the living room and watched My Three Sons and Bewitched. Then he took my sister off to put her to bed for the night.

Dad sat on the edge of my little sister's bed as I walked by the doorway towards my own room. She was eight years old. Peter Noone grinned down at them both from the poster above the head of the bed. Scores of stuffed animals surrounded her, from alligators to elephants to kittens. However, Weary Willy, the dilapidated floppy stuffed dog, was her favorite, and she held him in her left hand, rubbing her cheek with his tattered ear. Dad was tucking her in, and me as well, since my bedroom was next to hers and I could hear every word while I lay in bed pretending to read. Theoretically, I was too old to be tucked in, so I simply enjoyed from the next room.

"What do you want tonight, Snicklefritz? A song?"

"Yes. Sing for me, Papa. Please?" Dad broke into a soft rendition of Brahms's Lullaby in German. I always suspected he made up the German lyrics, but I later discovered they were quite accurate. When he reached the portion of the song that rose in pitch, the "Morgen früh," he crooned just a bit. My book lay across my chest at this point as I listened. After a moment, I heard my sister say sleepily, "Read me a story, okay?"

"Okay. What'll we read tonight?"

"This one." I waited to hear what story it might be.

"Okay, now lie down, hon. " Dad cleared his throat. "'Brer Rabbit had mo' trouble dan all de rest o' de animals in de forest. He need a whole bag o' tricks to keep out de way o' Brer Fox. An' one day it look de bag is empty." Dad read the Uncle Remus story of Brer Rabbit and the Laughing Place from the big story book that sat on my sister's bedside table. He was using his best deep south, old black man's accent. The book was a collection of stories that included Pecos Bill, Paul Bunyun, Johnny Appleseed, Uncle Remus, Casey at the Bat, Ichabod Crane, Davey Crockett, Mike Finn, and Hiawatha. I knew the book well: Walt Disney American Folklore. The green cover with illustrations around the edges had survived both my brothers as well as me, in addition to countless moves across the country. "...Yo done played yer las' trick on me, Brer Rabbit,' says Brer Fox. 'Yes sir, der ain't gon' to be no more tricks round her' unless dey is my tricks.' Brer Rabbit can't argufy wid dat." By today's standards, of course, it would be offensive to speak in such a stereo-typical fashion, but Dad certainly meant no harm. He simply imitated the accent used in the film. Sometimes he chose to read Pecos Bill, sometimes Casey at the Bat, which he recited as much as read, and sometimes one of the others, but Dad enjoyed reading the Remus stories the most, I think. Dad finished the story. "'Oh,' says Brer Rabbit, 'I didn't say it was yo'r laughin' place Brer Fox. I said it was MY laughin' place.' An' he start in laughin' all over agin til it look as if he kin hardly stand it." I heard the book close. "Good night, hon." I turned over my pillow to the cool side and lay my book on the floor.

"Read me this one too, Papa." Like every other child, she delayed. "I like this one."

"Okay. One more, then bedtime, okay?"

"Okay." I heard the music box play Little Brown Jug. Dad was reading "Goldilocks and the Three Bears and the Little Brown Jug of Sweet Honey." The story shifted the traditional tale into the bears stealing honey from a bees' nest and getting stung. At critical junctures of the story, the reader was to turn the crank, which played the melody of Little Brown Jug, and sing the lyrics from the book, extolling the wonders of honey early on, then lamenting the punishment from the bees later. Dad sang all the songs in a jovial voice. He finished up with the final song, cranking the melody as he sang: "Oh oh oh, I am sorry. Look at me and you'll agree, that it is not good for me, to take honey from the bees," then without the music, "unless, of course, I ask for it first." I heard to book close. "Okay, honey, it's time for bed." Then I heard their usual goodnights, said in unison: "Good night. Sleep tight. Don't let the bed bugs bite. See you in the morning. Good night. Sleep tight. And I love you." I heard the light switch, watched my Dad walk down the hallway, and I fell asleep.

Savory Corn Pudding

Serves 6-8.
Ingredients:
1/2 sweet onion, diced
3 tablespoons butter
1/2 teaspoon dried thyme, minced
1/2 teaspoon rosemary, minced
1 cup milk
2 eggs

1 teaspoon baking powder

1/2 cup self-rising yellow corn meal mix

1 teaspoon salt

1/4 teaspoon garlic powder

1 teaspoon Worcestershire sauce

1- 15 ounce can creamed corn

1/2 teaspoon sugar

ground black pepper to taste

1 1/2 cups cubed fresh bread

Several slices sharp cheddar cheese

Directions:

Preheat oven to 350°. In a medium skillet over medium-high heat, sauté onions and herbs in butter until the onions are translucent. Beat together the milk and eggs until thoroughly blended. In a large bowl mix onion mixture with all the other ingredients except cheese and stir well, adding the egg mixture last. Pour into a greased casserole dish and place cheese slices on top. Bake the casserole for about 45 minutes or until golden and set.

Stuffed Pork Chops

Serves 6

Ingredients:

¼ cup chopped celery

2 tablespoons butter

2 cups unseasoned stuffing mix

1 Granny Smith apple, diced; or 1 cup raisins; or 1 cup diced dried apricots

1 10 ½ ounce can chicken broth

2 teaspoons dried parsley flakes

Dash Worcestershire sauce
1 teaspoon salt
1/2 teaspoon paprika
1 teaspoon rubbed sage
½ teaspoon pepper
½ teaspoon dried thyme
6 pork loin chops (1 ½ inches thick)
½ cup dry white wine
6 slices sweet onion

Directions:

In a skillet, sauté celery in 1 tablespoon of butter until soft. Remove from the heat; stir in stuffing mix, ½ cup broth and seasonings; mix well. Cut a pocket in each pork chop by slicing from the fat side almost to the bone. Spoon about 1/2 cup stuffing into each pocket. Secure with string or toothpicks.

Melt remaining butter in a skillet. Brown the chops on both sides. Place in a greased 11-in. x 7-in. baking dish; pour remaining broth and wine over the chops and top each with a slice of onion and salt and pepper to taste. Cover and bake at 350° for 40-45- minutes or until juices run clear. Remove string or toothpicks before serving. Thicken pan juices if desired. Yield: 6 servings.

Taking Off

Dad gave me many presents over the years, the best ones intangible. One of the best presents he gave me was one he perhaps could not have seen coming, but it is one I have carried to this day.

It was 1968 and I had turned fifteen only a few weeks before. I had never flown before, and I certainly had never flown on my own. As a family, we had taken trains all up and down the eastern seaboard, and true baby- boomers, we had traveled across the country several times by car, but I had never flown.

My father raised me and my four siblings and by the time I was fifteen, I had not seen my mother in many years, so Dad drove me from the small western Kentucky town we lived in, across the river to the neighboring state, and to the airport some forty miles away so I could fly to New Orleans during spring break to visit with my mother. It was my father's Easter present to me. I wore a coat and tie, because flying in those days meant dressing the part. Secretly armed with my older brother's driver's license and a trove of misinformation about New Orleans from equally untraveled classmates, I eagerly awaited my great adventure. But truth be told, I worried about flying. Would we make it? Would I get air sickness? How would I find my way around the airports? Where would my luggage end up? As we navigated the two-lane roads in southern Indiana,

Dad recounted his own stories from his post-war years in New Orleans, anecdotes of fabulous food, romantic Spanish moss and the charm of the street cars. He told me warning tales about voodoo practices and gypsy card-readers and colorful street artists. He talked about the enticements of the French Quarters with its courtyards and wrought iron rails and exotic clubs. But he didn't talk much about flying. He knew I was nervous. He cut his eyes at my fidgeting and perhaps gave a little smirk, but he didn't say anything about it.

We arrived at the regional airport well before the flight, and he sat with me at the gate in the airport, which you could do back then. I was anxious, having no idea what it was like to fly, as well as not knowing just how this visit to see my mother might go after so many years. Dad watched me twitch, smiled, and patted me on the shoulder. When they called my flight, we stood up and I reached over to hug him goodbye, but instead of the familiar hug, he reached out and shook my hand, and said, "Enjoy your flight, son. I'll see you next week." Was this what it feels like to be grown? My father treated me like a peer, like an adult. My head swam a bit.

Heavy clouds passed over as we passengers boarded the plane by walking out onto the tarmac and climbing the steps that had been wheeled over to the propjet. The seats were far more spacious then, but my inspection of the seat pocket in front of me yielded no magazine or catalogue – just an air sickness bag and a safety card that I set about memorizing. The doors were pulled closed and the flight attendant gave her safety lesson, the one most of us can recite now, and I was both mesmerized and terrified. As she discussed the proper way to buckle up, I checked and rechecked my own seatbelt. I located the exits with my eyes, I made a note of the cover that would be doubtlessly dropping the air mask somewhere along the flight, and I wondered if there was any body of water between Indiana and Louisiana large enough for me to need the flotation device that was my seat. It began to rain.

The engines started up, the big propellers becoming a blur, and the plane started moving. My heart pounded. I had a window seat and watched us head down the taxiway. I looked for my father to be waving from a window of the terminal, but I couldn't see through the glass, and besides, he had turned around and headed for the Buick by the time I had checked through the gate. We gathered speed and the rain ran in streams across my window. I was aware of myself gripping the arm rests intensely, leaning forward, trying to remember the details of the safety talk just moments before. The engines whined a pitch higher and then, we were off the ground. I sat back now, still staring out the tiny window as we climbed up into the rain. We flew into the darkness of the clouds themselves, and still I watched the window. Suddenly, we came out above the clouds, and I was addicted to flying.

The entire world was cast in a brilliant white. I was soaring in the heavens and I was exhilarated. I had never experienced anything like it. My father had given me a gift I would forever cherish. I was free from the constraints of mere gravity. I was flying. All my nervousness disappeared and I felt joyous.

My mother met me at the airport and took me immediately to her favorite restaurant, a place near the lake. We travelled by street car. During my visit that week, she took me to the parts of New Orleans that many visitors don't see, the parts where people lived and worked and enjoyed life in the Big Easy. I also went on my own (remember, I had my brother's driver's license) to the French Quarter, and even treated myself to dinner at The Court of Two Sisters. But more important to me was I had had a wonderful adventure: flying. There was no doubt in my mind I would travel by plane again.

I flew back the next Saturday, a bright sunny day. I walked off the plane in the same coat and tie I had worn a week before and into the terminal where Dad was waiting for me, also in a sport coat and tie. The flight back had been just as exhilarating as the first flight. As I came through the gate, Dad reached out his hand and said, "Welcome home, son." I shook his hand and then gave him a long hug. The next day, Easter, I sat at the dinner table with my siblings, enjoying Dad's pineapple glazed ham, and they wanted to know about New Orleans and how my visit went with our mother, but it was difficult to stop talking about how amazing flying was. I had discovered a passion I would carry the rest of my life.

Since then, I have flown all over the world and visited amazing places and I do believe my love affair with travel began that rainy, early spring day, thanks to a very special gift from my father.

Dad's Easter Glazed Ham

Ingredients:
½ fully cooked ham
1 20-ounce can pineapple slices, juice reserved
15 to 20 whole cloves
1 small jar maraschino cherries
3/4 cup packed light brown sugar
2 tablespoons yellow mustard

Directions:
Preheat the oven to 350 degrees.

Place the ham in a large roaster, fat side up. Score the ham fat in opposite directions to create a diamond pattern in the ham. Arrange the pineapple slices on the scored ham, securing them with whole cloves. Place a cherry in the center of each pineapple ring and secure with a clove.

In a small bowl, combine the brown sugar, mustard and just enough of the reserved pineapple juice to make a thick glaze. Spoon the glaze over the ham and bake for 30-40 minutes. Remove the ham from the oven, transfer to a cutting board and carve.

Peccadillo

The colonel had been to the door before and left when I told him Dad wasn't home yet. He had stood before the doorway, his dress hat tucked under his arm, and listened intently when I explained that Dad had to stop by the grocery. It was information that I am sure was not needed, but it explained Dad's absence, and the colonel seemed to be interested. Colonel Sears then nodded and said he would return. I watched him retrace his way to the car, a government-issued Ford, and back down the driveway.

Colonel Sears, or "Ziggy," as we kids knew him, was a career man. We knew that but not much more, except that he was Rick's father and seemed to be gone quite a bit. But Ziggy was back now, ringing our doorbell. I saw him standing in exactly the same posture as he had stood earlier in the day, hat once again under his arm. Dad was home now and called for someone to open the door, but I was afraid. Rick and I, both fifteen, were often getting in trouble, and I knew this could not be good. Dad and Colonel Sears didn't even know each other, as far as I knew, so if he was calling for Dad, I must be in serious trouble. I watched him through a side window as he stood patiently before the door and I tried to recall just what manner of trouble Rick and I had been in lately. He rang the doorbell again.

"Answer the door!" Dad called from the kitchen, where exotic odors were being sent forth already. Peccadillo, one of Dad's favorites, full of spices and dried fruits. Dad had stopped for ingredients just to make this dish and I could smell the cinnamon and allspice. I pulled the door open slowly. Colonel Sears looked calm, not at all ready to discuss some transgression I might have committed.

"Your father home yet?" I considered lying, but I knew he had to have heard Dad yelling from the kitchen for someone to answer the door.

"Yes sir." I stood in the doorway, holding the door open a bit but not so much that Ziggy could see in.

"I need to speak with your father." He stepped towards the door and my choices were to either slam the door in his face or open it for him. I figured I had enough to worry about already and let him in and led him to the kitchen where Dad was measuring rice in a cup, standing before the sink in the kitchen island. Dad still had on his work shirt, a neatly pressed white one with creased short sleeves, but he looked downright casual next to the colonel, whose uniform was so wrinkle free he seemed permanently starched. For the first time since I had known him as Rick's father, I noticed just how deeply lined his face was. He wore an expression of seriousness, somberness. I guessed he was about the same age as Dad, maybe a bit younger, but he had a tired expression that made him look older. Dad put the pan on the stove and turned and looked at the colonel for the first time, and I saw Dad's face drop, his mouth open a bit, his eyes looking as if he couldn't quite focus.

"Mr. Weill, I'm Colonel Sears." He held his hand out. His left arm had the hat under it still. Dad wiped his hands on a towel and I could see they were shaking. He kept looking at Ziggy, but he didn't seem quite focused. Finally, Dad shook his hand. I stood in the dining room, watching these two giants just shaking each other's hands, slowly, carefully, eyes fixed on each other.

"Oh, shit," Dad finally said, and Ziggy reached out to steady him, my father, whom I had never seen needing a hand before ever, by gripping his forearm. Dad stared at him and regained his posture. It was as if they were pantomiming some sort of play I could not follow.

"Mr. Weill, I regret to inform you that your son, John Bruce Weill, died in service to his country." The colonel didn't move from his spot. Dad's eyes reddened. "Specialist Weill was killed by enemy fire on March twenty-fourth of this year in the Hua Nghia province of South Viet Nam." My thoughts tried to catch up to what was being said. My brother was dead. I tried to understand this news. As simple as it was, it didn't quite make sense. I had gotten a letter from Bruce only the day before. He was fine, wasn't he? Dad kept staring at Ziggy, and now tears started rolling down Dad's face. Behind him, the pot of rice was steaming furiously. I tried to take in this scene and understand, but could not quite do so. I ran to my room and buried my face in a pillow and sobbed, but what I kept seeing was my father's stricken face, suddenly gaunt, hollow, drained, vulnerable. I felt cowardly for having run out on him and got up to go help him, although what that might entail I did not have a clue. In the hallway, I met my other older brother who was running to the phone, his eyes streaming tears. I hadn't heard him come home, but he had been home long enough. I ran back to the kitchen where Dad was throwing away dinner, dumping rice down the food disposal, his movement jarring, angry, flailing. The sink was filled with steaming whiteness before the food went gurgling down the drain. Ziggy was still talking and I wanted to yell at him to stop it. Stop telling us this horrible news. Stop hurting my father. Stop killing my brother. His face seemed even more creased now, and his expression was subdued, solemn. I could only focus on phrases. " . . . disembarking from a helicopter . . . small arms fire . . . heroic . . . mortally wounded . . ." I didn't know it then, but that was all I would ever really know about my brother's death. The beef and raisins and spices were flying into the sink now, the water running full blast, the grinding non-stop. Dad's arms stopped grabbing now, and he leaned heavily against the sink, water on, motor whirring, and watched the food disappear. He reached up, turned off the disposal and the water and looked up at the colonel, who looked back, quiet now and so forlorn, I wanted to apologize, for some reason.

I heard a car door slam in the driveway, but I wasn't leaving my father again. Before the doorbell could sound, my brother let in my closest friend Jimmie and his sister and mother. My brother had called them. I'm not sure Jimmie's mother really knew my Dad, other than through occasional contacts regarding us kids, but she too was a single parent, and, a widow, she had had to cope with death. Jimmie's sister and my brother were close friends though. They came into the kitchen and the seven of us stood awkwardly in a loose gaggle of grief and support, the sink a tangle of tossed and now battered pots and lids. The colonel greeted Jimmie's mother with a nod, and again I think their acquaintance was pretty nebulous, and then told my Dad they could take care of details the next day. Dad looked a bit relieved, shook his hand and walked him to the door, but Dad's face looked vacant, empty.

We dined that night on a cardboard bucket of fried chicken, telling stories about my brother between bouts of crying and cursing and laughter. My younger sister was at Grandmother's and wouldn't know about this until later, but she was young enough that this would be different for her. I, however, was changed. My insular world had been closed in in a way I could not have seen, and I recall thinking even then that the colonel had what I would consider to be the worst job in the world, but one he performed with dignity. It was a long time before Dad cooked peccadillo again.

Dad's Peccadillo

Feeds 6
Ingredients:
1 pound of ground beef
1 onion, chopped
1 green pepper, chopped
2 cloves garlic, minced
2 tablespoons chili powder
1 teaspoon cinnamon
1 teaspoon ground cumin
½ teaspoon ground allspice
1/8 teaspoon ground cloves
1 teaspoon salt
¼ teaspoon black pepper
1/3 cup raisins
¼ cup pimiento-stuffed green olives (cut into halves)
½ cup slivered blanched almonds
1 4 ounce can tomato paste
½ cup water
A couple dashes of Worcestershire sauce
2 cups rice
4 cups water

Directions:

Cook beef until brown, then drain. Add onion, pepper, garlic. Cook until vegetables are tender. Add seasonings, raisins, olives, and almonds and cook briefly until spices are aromatic. Stir in tomato paste and water. Cover and cook over medium-low heat for 45 minutes.

Combine rice and water and cook over medium heat for 15 minutes, covered.

Combine meat mixture and cooked rice in a large bowl and press to mold into the shape of the bowl. Place a plate over the bowl and invert the bowl, tapping on the bowl to release the molded dish onto the plate.

Octopus Pizza

When Dad was drawing plans for shopping centers and nursing homes back in the 60's, all the drawing was not only done by hand, but the final set of plans was drawn in ink on vellum. These final drawings were then used to make blue print copies, a process I was familiar with primarily because of the overpowering ammoniacal smell of the blue print machine. Dad and his draftsman Joe would spend days carefully tracing the final plans from earlier pencil drawings, then letting the ink dry before continuing the tracing. It was a lengthy, painstaking process.

Joe had spent a week on the vellum drawing, working late the night before to finish so the ink would be dry when he came in the next morning. Dad went early to the drafting room and cut a piece of black construction paper into a free-form image of an ink spill, making sure to have one end narrower to imitate the flow ink would have running down the incline of the slanted drafting table. Then he took an empty ink bottle he had saved, cleaned, and dried for just this occasion. He carefully arranged the construction paper "spill" and the bottle at the top edge of Joe's weeklong project. Then Dad turned off the lights and went across the street for coffee.

When Joe drove up, Dad went to walk into work with him, chatting nonchalantly about some sporting event or television program from the night before. When Joe flipped on the fluorescent lights and looked at his table, he dropped his jacket and ran to the drawing. "Oh no! Oh no!" Joe picked up the bottle, saw the ruse, and shot Dad a look. Dad, meanwhile, clapped his hands at his waist and stooped forward and gave out a loud, "Ha!" followed by a grinning cackle of laughter afterwards.

Dad loved practical jokes and no one was immune to having one pulled on him. My wife had just met my father, who by this time had moved his office to his home. We were sitting in the cramped family room of the little house he had bought, Dad being the gracious southern gentleman he had been raised to be, when he looked at my wife and raised a finger in recollection. "Would you like a diamond pin?"

My wife was stunned. She barely knew my father. "A diamond pin? Why, thank you." Her blue eyes flew wide in anticipation. "How generous!" Dad stood and walked briskly into the business area of his house. Jennie turned to me. "Is he serious? What is it, some family heirloom?" I could only look at her unknowingly. My father was generous, but a diamond pin?

Dad came back with a small felt box and proudly handed it to my bride, who opened it expectantly. Inside was a safety pin attached through a hole in a dime. A dime-in-pin. Dad clapped his hands, leaned forward, and gave his characteristic, grinning, "Ha!"

Actually, he was legendary for his practical jokes, so pulling them off became more and more difficult as everyone was suspicious of him. As a result, props became a useful tool in his jokes. He had a doormat that would scream and yell, "Hey! Get off me!" when anyone walked in the door. He had fake eggs he would "accidently" drop on the floor at your foot as he fixed breakfast. There was a fake arm that hung from his car trunk on occasion. And one of his favorites was to walk into the room with his ever-present coffee cup in his hand that he would "spill" on his guest, although it was empty. When I actually put a few drops of water in a cup and "accidently" spilled it on him, and thus threw a tiny bit of water on him, he was not so amused. I told him, "Well, Pop, sometimes there has to be water in it for the joke to still work."

"Uh huh," he nodded. "You just wait." The look was a bit menacing. From then on, he would walk into the room with a full cup of horribly strong coffee and shoot me a glance. I don't think he ever threw water or coffee on me, but he kept the look up so I fully expected a cup of scalding coffee or cold water to dowse me any time I visited. It was, in his inimitable way, the best joke he pulled on me, the joke he only threatened and I kept expecting.

I often went to his office after school and did my homework or sometimes drew house designs on scrap paper. He and Joe and I would be engrossed in our endeavors, the room silent for long stretches of time. Then Pop would walk over to the row of catalogs he kept for specifying materials in a drawing, an innocent act that roused no suspicion, but then he would drop the heavy book flat on the tile floor and send a report through the office like a cannon going off, startling the Dickens out of Joe and me. I usually screamed (in a mature, manly way, despite my youth), but Joe only jumped then shook his head and went back to work while Pop laughed.

Pop enjoyed model railroading and although he never really found a spot to set up his entire train set, he still liked making the model buildings and creating mini-scenes that might be used one day in his set up. In a model hotel building, if you looked in the window, you would see a couple made of balsa in an amorous embrace in the bed.

Being an adventurous cook also led him to some gags. He brought home a plant someone gave him and asked me to grow it, since I liked gardening even as a child. It turns out it was an ornamental Thai pepper plant. When the tiny fruits turned red, I asked him what they tasted like. He plucked one from the plant, tossed it in his mouth, and made a face that told me it was delicious. "Oh, wow, they're actually sweet!" I picked a pepper and popped it in my mouth and ran to the kitchen with my mouth on fire while he clapped his hands together and laughed, the palmed pepper still in his hands. He did advise me to eat some bread and cool my mouth with milk, but it took me a long time to trust his taste buds again. But most of his culinary surprises were not of the spicy pepper type. He loved to prepare dishes that people would love, and then tell them what they were eating. There was the braised beef heart, roasted beef tongue, and eggs with pork brains (which sent my sister to the bathroom), among other delicacies, all of which I learned to like before I knew what they were. When we were teenagers with friends over, Dad liked to fix octopus pizza, which was amazingly delicious, so he could see the look on their faces when it was revealed. We would not let on, the revelation of ingredients being Pop's domain. Our friends' expressions when he answered their question, "Wow, this is great! What is it?" with "Octopus" was too good to miss. And while they may have looked puzzled and astounded, they did not stop eating. Meanwhile, Dad would clap his hands and give out with a big, "Ha!" enjoying the surprise.

His penchant for pulling off the joke he actually used in his drawing of designs. He became something of an expert in designing church buildings. One item he always included in the vestibule between the nave and the Sunday school building was a thermostat that was connected to nothing. The building committee or pastor might question why it was present, and he would tell them, "People all have different temperatures and they want to control the air in the room. This way, people can turn up the heat or crank up the air conditioner and they will THINK they are making it warmer or cooler. If they think they are, they are generally happy." The thermostat always stayed in the design. When I was a child and would occasionally accompany my father on construction site inspections, I always looked for the fake thermostat.

Octopus Pizza

Feeds 4-6 adventurous eaters
DOUGH
Two 12-inch crusts
Combine in a large bowl and let stand until the yeast is dissolved, about 5 minutes:
1 1/3 cups warm (105° to 115°F) water
1 package (2 1/4 teaspoons) active dry yeast

Add:
3 1/2 to 3 3/4 cups all-purpose flour, starting with 2 cups
2 tablespoons olive oil
1 teaspoon salt
1 tablespoon sugar

Mix by hand for about 1 minute, stirring vigorously. Knead on a floured board for 10 full minutes, adding the remaining flour. Transfer the dough to a bowl lightly coated with olive oil and turn it once to coat with oil. Cover with plastic wrap or a clean cloth and let rise in a warm place (75° to 85°F) until doubled in bulk, 1 to 1 1/2 hours. Preheat the oven to 450°F.

Grease 2 baking sheets and dust with cornmeal. Punch down the dough and divide it in half. Roll each piece into a ball and let rest, loosely covered with plastic wrap, for 10 to 15 minutes.

One at a time, flatten each ball of dough on a lightly floured work surface into a 12-inch round, rolling and stretching the dough. Don't worry about making it perfectly round. Leaving it oddly shaped makes it rustic. Place each patted out pie on a prepared baking sheet. Lift the edges and pinch to form a lip. To prevent the filling from making the crust soggy, brush the top of the dough with olive oil

Use your fingertips to push dents in the surface of the dough, to prevent bubbling, and let rest for about 10 minutes.

FILLING:
Drain 2 4-ounce cans octopus packed in oil.

Cut the octopus into medium-sized pieces leaving tendrils intact and set aside.

Sauté 5 minced garlic cloves in olive oil for about five minutes until garlic is tender and aromatic. Add 1 can tomato paste, ½ cup water, ½ cup red wine, 1 tablespoon basil, 1 tablespoon oregano, 1 teaspoon Worcestershire, ¼ teaspoon cayenne, 1 tablespoon sugar, salt and pepper to taste. Cook uncovered for 10 - 15 minutes until the sauce has thickened.

To make the pizza, divide the filling between the two crusts and lay the drained octopus on the sauce. Top with mozzarella cheese and bake in a 450 degree oven until hot and bubbly in the middle and the crust is browned a bit 10-15 minutes.

Beef Tongue Pot Roast with Onion Gravy

Serves: 4

Pop always used a stove top pressure cooker. I have adjusted it for an Instant Pot.

Ingredients:
Beef Tongue
2 large beef tongues
1 large yellow onion, quartered
6 cloves garlic
3 tablespoons kosher salt
2 tablespoon whole black peppercorns
4 bay leaves
2 teaspoons dried thyme

Onion Gravy
2 tablespoons butter
1 tablespoon olive oil
1 large sweet onion, halved and thinly sliced
4 cloves garlic, minced
½ teaspoon dried thyme
3 tablespoons all-purpose flour
3 cups beef broth
Salt and pepper

Instructions:
Wash the tongues thoroughly and place into the pressure cooker with remaining seasonings. Cover with water and cook on high temperature for 90 minutes. Let the pressure release naturally until the pin drops. Remover the tongues and place

them in an ice water bath until just cool enough to handle. Peel the tongues and trim. Discard the skin. Slice the tongue thinly and set aside.

Meanwhile, make the gravy: In a large skillet, melt butter in the olive oil over medium heat. Add the onion, and cook, stirring frequently, until soft and turning clear, 8 to 10 minutes. Add garlic and thyme and cook until aromatic, about 1 minute. Add the flour and cook, stirring constantly, for 3 minutes. Add the beef broth and bring to a simmer, stirring frequently, until the sauce thickens. Season to taste.

Add the sliced beef tongue. Reduce the heat to medium-low, cover, and simmer until the flavors have married, about 10 minutes.

Dad served this with either egg noodles or mashed potatoes.

Brains with Scrambled Eggs

Yield: 6 servings (if you can find six willing souls)
Ingredients:
1 pound pork brains
3 tablespoons butter or margarine
Salt and pepper
8 eggs
¼ cup milk

Instructions:
Wash brains thoroughly in cold running water, carefully removing membrane. Drain in a colander well, then chop roughly.

Sauté the brains in butter in a large skillet until it changes to a whitish color. Try not to break up the brains too much. Season with salt and pepper. Combine eggs and milk and beat

well. Stir into brains and cook over medium heat, stirring frequently, until eggs are firm but still moist. Serve immediately.

No Money for Butter

We four kids were giddy. It was the first day of our family vacation, a two-week adventure that Dad had carefully planned as he did each year, allowing us to see America a little bit more each year. We had traveled to Civil War sites, to Florida, to our nation's capitol, and even to Disney Land in California. This year, we were heading for San Antonio and something called a HemisFair, which would turn out to be fabulous. But this first day, we had driven part of the way and had stopped at a Ramada Inn for the night.

It must be understood that staying in motels en route was something of a rarity. Dad was one of those men who would roust us out of bed at 2 a.m. to start vacation so we could arrive at our destination all the sooner, in one day, if possible. I remember vividly the odd feeling of crossing state lines in the dark, trying to keep a record of it in my diary. It wasn't unusual for us to be in our third or fourth state by the end of a single day of driving. But it was early yet, the sun still out and the day warm, and we had already stopped at a Ramada Inn. The exciting part for us kids was the pool, of course.

We had tumbled out of the Buick (and it was always a Buick, for Dad), scrambled to our rooms with our suitcases, and changed into swimsuits in a flash. Motivation is a wonderful thing. We would sit motionless for hours watching television instead of doing the first chore, but the prospect of swimming in the motel pool had us moving like dervishes. Dad wanted us to put our suitcases away and act in a vaguely civilized manner, but when we went running past him, he just waved us by and gave a smile. That smile was more devious upon reflection than I recognized at the time. "Keep an eye on your sister," was all he offered us.

Three brothers splashing and raising a ruckus and our sister, the youngest, tagging along behind every step, brought a great deal of energy in the pool. There were other families there too, of course: young parents with children even younger than us bouncing in the shallow end; baby boomer families, with teenaged sons and daughters that we eyed with both suspicion and interest as they practiced dives from the board or came pushing up from the water with long tresses down their backs; older couples who sat in the poolside furniture cluck-clucking us as we raced around with abandon. Okay, we were probably overly rowdy – brothers especially have a way of inspiring such behavior.

Dad would not have approved our raucousness, but he wasn't there yet. We had left him in the room. Where was he, anyway? Then he came out and we all stopped.

There was our Dad, professional man, businessman, war veteran, strolling along the balcony of the Ramada Inn with a towel over his arm, wearing the skimpiest Speedo I had ever seen. His legs, which never, ever saw sunlight, were blinding white. His woven huarache sandals (where had he hidden those?) flipped along the concrete as he walked jauntily towards the stairway. His facial expression was a practiced debonair smirk, his head cocked to one side, an eyebrow raised ever so slightly.

We were, of course, humiliated. Here was our father in a Speedo, casting glances surreptitiously at the women around the pool as the sauntered to a chair, tossed his towel and horn-rimmed glasses nonchalantly onto a small table beside it, then ambled towards the diving board. We were aghast. How could he? It is true that most eyes were on him – although we have all been warned about looking into the sun. His legs were just screaming white. He stepped onto the board, strode purpose-fully towards the end with measured steps, and made a per-fect swan dive.

We didn't see him come up. We had already scattered to our rooms, embarrassed beyond belief, by the time he surfaced.

Like most children, because our Dad was our Dad, a dif-ferent generation, in our eyes he was always middle aged. It was always surprising to us when he demonstrated the youth-fulness and vigor of a man in his prime. I recall playing pitch and catch with my older brother in the driveway of our home. As it often happened, what began as a game tossing the ball and making muted crowd noises as if we were winning the pennant with that particular catch turned into a game of "burn out," which is when teenaged boys try to see who is tougher by see-ing who can hurt the other's hand by pitching the ball as hard as possible. Because my brother and I were very close in size and age, and because we were stubborn teenaged boys (yes, that is redundant), neither of us would give, although both of us had very sore hands. About that time, Dad came home from work, immediately sized up the situation, and asked if he could throw one pitch. Sure, we answered. How quaint that the old man wanted to throw the baseball with us. My brother crouched in a catcher's stance and held his glove in an imaginary strike zone. We figured it would be a gentle, friendly toss, the kind seen when some elderly celebrity tosses the first pitch at the Senator's game. Dad leaned forward, looked into my brother's glove, and stood back in the stretch. He glanced furtively to his left to keep the non-existent runner close to a non-existent first base. Was it possible our father knew what a baseball was? He wound up and hummed a pitch so hard we could scarcely see it. My brother fell to the side just as the ball whizzed past him and buried itself into the garage door.

"You moved!" Dad gawked at the hole in the door.

"Uh, yeah." Ernie and I looked back and forth at each other incredulously. The man still had it. I asked Ernie later why he moved, and he told me, "I had a vision of a bb being shot through a marshmallow. I was the marshmallow."

Dad shrugged and went into the house to make pork chops Provençale for dinner. That hole in the garage door, a perfect strike, by the way, remained until we moved many years later, a reminder to us that perhaps Dad was not quite ready for the retirement home.

To be clear, Dad always pushed back against getting old. He might have to age, he told me once, but that did not mean he had to grow old. His methods were sometimes those that one might expect of a man who turns fifty or fifty-five or sixty, but Dad had a certain style about his push-backs that made them his. By my math, he was forty-five when The Speedo Event (as we thereafter called it) occurred. Five years later, when the sixties had just finished and Dad turned fifty, he refused to go gently.

Dad's sons had brought the '60's full steam into our home, although my oldest brother had already died in Viet Nam. Perhaps that is what helped him become a quiet supporter of the counter culture that I embraced in my teen years. He was against the war, which I found a great many in my father's generation were also against, but he also developed a disdain for authority which was almost visceral. I actually watched my father walk up to a restaurant booth full of Kentucky state troopers and give them the raspberry. I think they were so surprised to see a man of his age and stature in the community razzing them, they could only stare with utter surprise. It was shortly after that Dad started giving soul handshakes when he met business prospects or when he closed a meeting at work. I was away at college when he started doing that and I came home for a visit. I sat in Dad's office while he went over some drawings or negotiated a deal. As the contractor or property owner rose to leave and offered a hand, Dad reached over and grabbed the person's thumb, gripped it, and held the gripped hands with his left hand. I half expected him to start talking jive. I just sat there, watching these people trying to figure out what he was doing. They would move their hands up or down to negotiate the position of Dad's hand, or attempt to shake the new grip as if it were a traditional handshake, which always failed. They always looked completely ill-at-ease, but Dad never seemed to notice. Dad was a five foot six businessman with a Jewish heritage. He was not a brother. As it turned out, his repeat customers started to anticipate Dad's soul handshake and it was surreal to watch the plumbing contractor and the architect standing in the middle of the office in a soul shake, exchanging pleasantries. When I later told Dad that the times had changed and the soul handshake was now passé, he gave it up, but not without some remorse. Ironically, his return to a traditional handshake thoroughly confused those men whom he had converted.

Turning sixty-five was a bigger challenge for Dad. Dad had had a bald spot on his head since I can remember, a perfectly round hairless circle looking like a yarmulke on his head. He tried comb-overs and comb-backs, but, of course, the spot grew. By the time he was sixty-five, it was the better part of his head. So Dad did what none of us expected: he started wearing a toupée. But of course, Dad didn't just get a regular hairpiece. No, he bought one that honestly looked like flattened, very fuzzy road kill. It was quite different from what was left of his real hair so it sometimes looked like a squirrel was nesting on him. And the toupée wasn't the only change. He also chucked the black, horn-rimmed shower-door-thick glasses he had worn since the fifties in favor of some very seventies steel-rimmed glasses. Then, to top off the metamorphosis, he traded in his last Buick for a Pontiac Fiero, which Dad always mispronounced so it sounded like he was saying he drove a Ferrari. I strongly suspect he knew the correct pronunciation.

I had said Dad was a Buick man. I should explain his move to a Pontiac, beyond the fact it was little sports car. He had traded with the same dealer for years, always bringing home a somewhat bigger, fancier sedan every four years or so until they sold him a lemon. Dad took it back innumerable times, but it just never was quite right, with engine lights popping on and off, transmission problems, brake issues, the whole car just acting as if it had a grudge against Dad. He tried to get them to take it back, but they refused. He kept that car for the duration of his payments, paying the final payment with a huge bag of pennies. He never drove another Buick.

I can still see Dad in is "Frarari," steelies glinting, the squirrel nestled on his head as he drove off to the club he called The Menopause Lounge, looking for an evening of romance. It was proof he wasn't old yet.

Pork Chops Provençale

Serves 8, unless you have three teenaged sons, then serves 5.

Ingredients:

8 pork chops

1 yellow onion, diced

1 cup diced celery

½ cup diced carrots

2 garlic cloves, crushed

1 can tomato paste + 1 can of water

1 tablespoon cider vinegar

1 tablespoon brown sugar

1 tablespoon Worcestershire sauce

1 tablespoon (or more) Herbs de Provence

1 teaspoon dry mustard

1 teaspoon paprika

Salt and pepper to taste

Directions:

In a pressure cooker bottom, brown chops in olive oil on each side. Add onion, celery and carrots and cook until onions are golden. Add the garlic and cook another minute. Add tomato paste and remaining ingredients and seal top of cooker. Cook under pressure for 30-40 minutes then release the pressure. Serve with cottage fries.

Cottage Fries

Serves 5-6
Ingredients:
2 tablespoons butter
1 tablespoon vegetable oil
4 medium potatoes (1 1/4 pound), thinly sliced
¼ teaspoon salt
⅛ teaspoon garlic powder
1/4 teaspoon pepper
1 small yellow onion, thinly sliced and separated into rings

Directions:
In a large skillet with a close-fitting lid melt butter in the oil. (If necessary, add additional butter or oil during cooking.) Layer potatoes into skillet. Sprinkle with salt, garlic powder, and pepper. Cook, covered, over medium heat for 10-12 minutes. Add onion rings. Cook, uncovered, for 8-10 minutes more or until potatoes are tender and browned, turning frequently. To speed the process up, Dad often would use leftover baked potatoes that he had intentionally cooked too many of for another meal. If using already baked potatoes, cook together with the seasonings and onion rings for 8-10 minutes over medium heat, turning frequently.

Stuffed Peppers

Serves 6
Ingredients:
1 pound ground beef
1/2 cup uncooked long grain white rice
1 cup water
6 large green bell peppers
2 (6 ounce) cans tomato paste
1 ½ cups water
Splash of dry red wine
1 ½ tablespoons Worcestershire sauce
½ teaspoon garlic powder
½ teaspoon onion powder
salt and pepper to taste
2 teaspoons Italian seasoning
½ teaspoon sugar
1 cup shredded Monterey jack cheese

Directions
Preheat oven to 350 degrees F

Place the rice and water in a sauce pan, and bring to a boil. Reduce heat, cover, and cook 20 minutes. In a skillet over medium heat, break up and cook the beef until evenly browned. Drain the fat.

Remove and discard the tops, seeds, and membranes of the bell peppers. Arrange peppers in an oiled baking dish with the hollowed sides facing upward.

Add to the drained meat in the skillet the remaining ingredients except the cheese and cook on medium-low heat for several minutes.

In a bowl, mix the beef mixture and the cooked rice. Spoon an equal amount of the mixture into each hollowed pepper. Top each with shredded Monterey jack cheese. Cover with foil.

Bake 1 hour in the preheated oven, then remove foil and bake an additional 10-15 minutes until cheese is bubbly.

Moveable Feasts

"It only costs a nickel more to go first class," Dad used to say. As a child, I took that far too literally, but I have since learned what he meant: It is sometimes a wise purchase to spend more for something of value to you. While he was not by any means a spendthrift, having gone through The Great Depression, there were times he would splurge, usually around The Big Three holidays (as we called them): Easter, Thanksgiving, and Christmas. And because he loved to cook, Dad's "nickel more" most often went towards great meals.

For our religious training, Dad took us kids to Zion United Church of Christ. It was a German church with a blonde-headed Jesus staring up into the holy light of the garden in the stained-glass window at the front of the apse. The building itself was brick and stone and my recollection of it is fond. Dad would drive us over for Sunday school, drop us off, then meet us for the regular service in just over an hour. I always supposed he went to the counter at the back of Weir's Drug Store nearby for a cup of coffee and to read the Sunday Messenger-Inquirer in peace and quiet. We usually sat in the back section of the sanctuary, along with a woman who always sat behind us who evidently believed she was a doxology away from being discovered by the Metropolitan Opera Company. We boys wore sport coats and ties, my sister a dress. I believe for the most part, we were pretty well behaved, but the tradition of the church in my memory was for the pastor to bring up issues of faith and put forth a reasoned point of view concerning those issues. For me as a child, that meant a dry service. We loved the music and we made friends in Sunday school, but the service was most definitely adult oriented. Yet we attended fairly regularly, sitting next to Dad, my shoulder aching mysteriously from sitting still so long and trying not to squirm. When Dad started folding up a dollar into a tiny square for the offering tray, we knew we were near the end of the service.

Despite this outward show, Dad was not a highly religious man. He believed, but his attendance at church was more for our benefit than that of his soul. When we grew older, he sometimes would take us to Sunday school and then pick us up afterwards (discreetly around the corner from the front door of the church) and take us home. I am not sure just when we stopped going completely. But Dad still had faith that was borne out in our celebration of holidays.

The Big Three were Easter, Thanksgiving, and Christmas, and their significance was in reverse order of their occurrence on the calendar. We celebrated other holidays, of course, just not in an extravagant, organized way. We might stay up late on New Year's Eve, but it was pretty subdued. We bought boxes of valentines for the school party, pinched each other on St. Patrick's Day if we did not have on something green, and we sometimes would have a picnic on Memorial Day, but the last one usually depended upon whom Dad was dating at the time. I don't have any memory of going to downtown Owensboro for fireworks on the Fourth of July, although I am sure they had them, and all we did for Labor Day was maybe a trip to the lake for swimming, but usually with our friends rather than family. Even birthdays, while they came with some presents to be opened at the dinner table and a rarely kept rule that our siblings had to be nice to us, were not overly big occasions. Although Pop would make a pineapple upside down cake for us on our birthdays. But with The Big Three, Dad built traditions and would open his wallet some.

Easter came first, and it was marked with coloring eggs using tablets of dye and vinegar in coffee cups, then Dad hiding them late the night before Easter, with the egg in the milk glass nesting hen always left for our little sister to find. Occasionally, eggs remained unfound and noxiously gave themselves up only after a few days. There was always a basket hidden for each child, usually employing rattan paper plate holders and plastic green grass, with assorted marshmallow chicks, jelly beans, and cream-filled eggs. A chocolate bunny was in it as well. All of this candy was unusual for us, since we rarely ate sweets and almost never had desserts growing up. Theoretically, we were through with Lent, but if we had given up anything, it was lost on me. After the hunt was the Easter service at Zion, bedecked with lilies, where the usually somber minister cranked it up a notch and brought in a timpani player and a French horn to give punctuation to his reading of the gospel. The soprano auditioner behind us also made sure to up it a notch as well. Then it was home for the Easter feast. We knew it was serious because Dad always changed into casual cooking clothes for the preparations.

Nearly every year, it was a huge ham glazed with mustard, brown sugar, and pineapple slices with cherries in the center. Easter eggs were readily donated for the accompanying deviled eggs. Mashed potatoes, gravy, salad, green beans, perhaps a Jello salad, Dad fixed them all. Our grandmother would come over and we would sit for dinner using the lace table cloth that was used exactly three times a year and Dad would give the blessing, which was the same blessing he gave each meal, but this time said more slowly and with feeling.

Thanksgiving was embraced even more than Easter at Dad's table. While there were not the accompanying religious events Easter had, the traditions remained. First off, Dad always bought the largest turkey he could find. We are talking at least thirty pounds of poultry here. The size was predicated on the fact that my oldest brother, who was quite thin, would eat an entire leg quarter with his meal. And afterwards, there were meals for the next week: turkey slices with gravy and cranberries, turkey sandwiches, turkey hash using dressing, turkey a la king, turkey tetrazzini, turkey casserole, and, ultimately, turkey and rice soup made from boiling the carcass which had been picked nearly clean. The Thanksgiving meal itself included a host of Dad's traditional favorites, including apple-walnut dressing, creamed onions, cranberry sauce, sweet potatoes, green beans, and scalloped oysters. Bowls of cornichons, black olives, and stuffed celery also adorned the lace table cloth and Dad would call us from the football game on television and he would positively beam over the spread. Then, he would say the same blessing, again slowly and meaningfully, and we would dive in. It was truly an epicurean celebration. If we stopped eating, he would say, "You didn't like it," and look dejected. But that was never the case, and we sometimes ate until we literally rolled out of our chairs to finish watching the Cowboys and promptly fall asleep.

But Christmas was a step above in every way. The tree came first, and we usually bought ours from a lot by the shopping center far too near to Thanksgiving, so that the dried out needles were embedded in the carpeting for months once we had taken the tree down. Shopping for the tree was an event for the family, so Dad would load everyone into the Buick and drive us the lot to inspect what was available. Dad tended towards spruces. Once home, he would attach the holder and place the tree in its prominent spot and then string the lights around it, thwacking the bulbs along the way to ensure proper operation. Then the boxes of decorations: brightly colored glass balls that diminished in number each year; handmade construction paper garlands we kids had made in school, faded from the years; various mismatched trinkets that had been given as presents, usually by women Dad knew, made from glued sea shells or corncobs and sporting the name of a vacation destination; and small metallic stars and snowflakes from a bygone time. Sometimes we would cut out paper snowflakes and add them, if we were feeling industrious. We always ended with a layer of silver tinsel that gave the tree an ethereal glow when the lights were on and the house was dark. All of these final decorations were applied by the kids while Dad sat in a chair, pointing out gaps in the coverage, sipping a glass of wine. Once we kids had finished, Dad took the glass spire topper and placed atop the tree, and we would sit back and bask in its light and start building our anticipation.

Christmas shopping was a family affair as well. We would go together downtown for the annual Christmas parade the weekend after Thanksgiving. Local high school bands marched along, playing the few songs they had learned for the event. Boy Scouts trooped along in a string of tan outfits. Flatbed floats pulled by pick-up trucks and tractors held carefully constructed, chicken-wire and crepe paper snow men, piles of brightly wrapped boxes and small groups of people whose presence I never quite grasped, waving and tossing candy towards the crowd. Convertibles with local celebrities, from mayor to beauty queen, idled by. When the parade was over, we would scatter with friends across downtown to begin shopping for the holidays. The Salvation Army booth at the corner of Second and Daviess was manned with bell ringers and Kiwanians selling fruitcakes. Dad dropped money in the bucket and bought a fruitcake each year. The streets bustled with holiday cheer and, in the safety of an earlier time, we kids wandered freely. Eventually we would end up at the diner near the bridge, enjoying an open-faced roast beef sandwich, with wonderful globs of brown salty gravy covering the mashed potatoes and white bread. During the rest of the year, Dad was not given to impulse buying or the accumulation of possessions, but during Christmas, he splurged. He insisted, first of all, on a list from each of us, and it was only much later that I learned not to be demur in my list because if it was on the list, we generally got it.

There was one year in particular that stands out in the realm of presents. We had only recently moved to a new neighborhood with Dad and our first step mother (there would be more), and because of her desire to win us over and the fact that we had lost most of our possessions in a previous move, it was an extravaganza. Even as adults, we still refer to it as "That Christmas." We were kept from entering the living room until we could all enter at once, which was different but not too much so. When we went in, the room was overflowing with gifts: bicycles for everyone, models, cars, dolls, games, wrist watches – everything. I can still recall my chemistry set, the puppet theater with hand-puppets of Snow White and the Seven Dwarves, the model T-Bird to be assembled, my silver-colored Timex, and the shiny green Schwinn that I learned to ride on.

Each year we put out a sock Christmas Eve that Dad filled with nuts, tangerines and oranges, ribbon hard candy (which always came out a bit linty), and yet another small present. The distribution of gifts was done in a deliberate fashion, with one of us receiving a gift from under the tree and opening it for all to see before the next gift was handed out. We lolled around the tree, opening presents and eating fruits and candy all morning. The Firestone Collection of Christmas Classics played in the background while Dad drank coffee and watched, still in his bathrobe, his chin stubbly. Our grandmother would have spent the night and she would always chide Dad mildly for his extravagance, but he would simply smile at her and look back towards his family spread before him.

I am sure we must have had a sandwich or something for lunch, but I cannot bring it to mind because what I remember of Christmas dining was that Dad would start in late morning and prepare wondrous menus to celebrate the day. Unlike Easter and Thanksgiving, the meals varied. Sometimes we had a ham, but there were many others. Once we had a barbequed venison shoulder. Another time we had a leg of lamb with mint jelly, which Dad considered a fine eating combination if ever there was one. There were stuffed pork roasts with port wine reductions and rib roasts au jus. One of my favorites was Dad's duck a l'orange, with the perfectly crisped skin and the citrusy, savory sauce. Of course, each of the meats was always accompanied by a host of vegetable dishes and fruit compotes. Grandmother would help some, although usually by keeping us kids out of the way as much as any other way. I rarely saw her imbibe in drink, perhaps the occasional beer, but each Christmas, as Dad was finishing the preparations, she would join him a short glass of straight Kentucky bourbon.

The lace tablecloth was brought forth and the feast was laid out. The antique silverware, the Enoch Woods blue transferware Dad had inherited, and platters of food filled the table. Dad said the blessing with meaning again, and we would allow our taste buds to be thrilled with the delights. And it only cost a nickel more.

Pineapple Upside Down Cake

Ingredients:
12 pineapple slices with juice reserved (three 8-oz cans)
16 maraschino cherries
3 tablespoons butter, melted
½ cup packed brown sugar
1 box yellow cake mix
1 cup reserved pineapple juice (from can of pineapple)
½ cup vegetable oil
3 eggs

Directions:
Heat oven to 350°F. Add melted butter to 12-inch cast iron skillet. Sprinkle brown sugar evenly over butter. Arrange 8 pineapple slices in bottom of skillet. Cut remaining slices in half; arrange around inside edge of skillet. Place 1 cherry in center of each whole and half pineapple slice.

In large bowl, beat cake mix, pineapple juice, oil and eggs with electric mixer on low speed until moistened; beat 2 minutes on high speed. Pour into skillet over fruit.

Bake 40 to 45 minutes or until cake is golden brown and springs back when touched lightly in center.

Cool cake in skillet 5 to 10 minutes. Run knife around edge of cake to loosen. Place heatproof plate upside down over skillet; turn plate and skillet over. Remove skillet. Serve cake warm.

Scalloped Oysters

Serves 4
Ingredients:
8 tablespoons cold butter, cut into small pieces
1 quart oysters, drained
2 cups saltine cracker crumbs
1/4 teaspoon ground nutmeg
salt and pepper, to taste
1/4 cup whipping cream
Dash Worcestershire

Directions:
Lightly butter a 1 1/2 to 2-quart casserole dish. Set aside a few cracker crumbs and 1 tablespoon of butter for topping. Cover the bottom of the dish with some of the cracker crumbs then top with a layer of oysters, a layer of crumbs, and some of the butter pieces. Repeat layers until all oysters are used. Season with the salt, pepper and nutmeg. Mix the cream and Worcestershire and pour over the dish then top with reserved crumbs and butter. Bake in a preheated 375 degree oven for about 30 minutes, or until heated and browned. Serve immediately.

Apple Walnut Dressing

Serves 6-8
Ingredients:
2 tablespoons butter
1/2 cup onions, diced
1/2 cup celery, diced
1 1/2 cups apples, diced
1 cup apple juice
1 can chicken broth
3 teaspoons dried crushed sage
Ground black pepper to taste
1/2 cup English walnuts, chopped
5 cups seasoned stuffing mix

Directions:
In a large skillet over medium heat sauté onions and celery in butter until tender. Add apples and sauté briefly for 3-4 minutes. Add apple juice and simmer 7-8 minutes. Add chicken broth and return to a boil; remove from heat and add the sage and pepper. In a large mixing bowl combine apple mixture and walnuts with stuffing; mix well until completely moistened. Place in a shallow, non-stick baking dish and bake at 350° for 7 to 10 minutes or until golden brown.

Pop's Deviled Eggs (updated just a bit)

Makes 12 deviled eggs

This is my memory of Pop's deviled eggs. I have updated it by using an Instant Pot to boil the eggs. Once you have cooked hard boiled eggs in an Instant Pot and found them amazingly easy to peel, you won't go back.

Ingredients:
6 large eggs
3 tbsp salad dressing (such as Miracle Whip)
1 tsp yellow mustard
1 tsp sweet pickle juice
Dash hot sauce (such as Crystals) or sprinkle of cayenne
Salt and pepper, to taste
Paprika, for garnish

Instructions:
Place the eggs on the metal basket provided with the Instant Pot. Add one cup water, then set on manual for four minutes. Let the pressure release naturally for four minutes.

While the eggs are boiling prepare an ice water bath and set aside.

After the eggs have released naturally for four minutes, do a quick release for the remaining pressure. Remove the eggs with tongs and place immediately into the ice water bath.

Once the eggs have cooled completely, peel them and slice in half lengthwise. Remove the yolk to a small bowl with a spoon and place the egg whites on a plate.

Mash the yolks with a fork and add the next five ingredients. Stir everything together.

Using a spoon, add a portion of the deviled egg mixture back into the hole of each egg white, overfilling each by half an inch. Sprinkle on paprika for garnish.

Duck a l'Orange

Serves 8
Ingredients:

For duck:
2 tablespoons kosher salt
2 teaspoons ground coriander
1 teaspoon ground cumin
2 teaspoon black pepper
2 (5 to 7 lb) Pekin ducks
2 juice oranges, halved
8 fresh thyme sprigs
8 fresh marjoram sprigs
4 fresh flat-leaf parsley sprigs
1 large sweet onion, cut into 12 wedges
1 cup dry white wine
1 cup chicken stock
1 carrot, halved
1 celery rib, halved

For sauce:
1/2 cup sugar
1/2 cup fresh orange juice
3 tablespoons white-wine vinegar
1/4 teaspoon salt
6 tablespoons chicken stock

1 ½ tablespoon butter, softened

1 ½ tablespoon all-purpose flour

1 ½ tablespoon fresh orange zest in strips

Instructions:

Roast duck:

Put oven rack in middle position and preheat oven to 475°F.

Stir together salt, coriander, cumin, and pepper. Pat ducks dry and sprinkle inside and out with spice mixture. Cut 1 orange into quarters and put half in each duck cavity with thyme, marjoram, parsley, and 3 onion wedges.

Squeeze juice from remaining orange and stir together with wine and stock. Set aside.

Spread remaining onion wedges in large flame-proof roasting pan with carrot and celery halves, then place ducks on top of vegetables and roast 30 minutes.

Pour wine mixture into roasting pan and reduce oven temperature to 350°F. Continue to roast duck until thermometer inserted into a thigh (close to but not touching bone) registers 170°F, 1 to 1 1/4 hours more. Turn on broiler and broil duck 3 to 4 inches from heat until top is golden brown, about 3 minutes. Be careful not to overbrown the ducks.

Tilt the ducks to drain juices from cavity into pan and transfer ducks to a cutting board, reserving juices in pan. Tent the ducks with foil and let stand 15 minutes.

Make sauce:

While duck roasts, cook sugar in a dry 1-quart heavy saucepan over moderate heat, undisturbed, until it begins to melt. Continue to cook, stirring occasionally with a fork, until sugar melts into a deep golden caramel. Add orange juice, vinegar, and salt (use caution; mixture will bubble and steam vigorously) and simmer over low heat, stirring occasionally, until caramel is dissolved. Remove syrup from heat.

Discard vegetables from roasting pan and pour pan juices through a fine-mesh sieve into a 1-quart glass measure or bowl, skim off and discard fat. A fat separator works well for this. Add enough stock to pan juices to total 1 1/2 cup liquid.

Stir together butter and flour to form a ball (beurre manié.) Bring pan juices to a simmer in a 2-quart heavy saucepan, then add beurre manié, whisking constantly to prevent lumps. Add orange syrup and zest and simmer, whisking occasionally, until sauce is thickened slightly and zest is tender, about 5 minutes. Serve with ducks.

Leg of Lamb with Potatoes and Mint Jelly

Serves 7-8
<u>Ingredients</u>
For lamb and potatoes:
1 lamb leg, roughly 6-7 pounds
2 stalks fresh rosemary, stripped
6 medium potatoes, peeled and quartered
4 tablespoons olive oil
Salt and pepper

For mint jelly:
1 cup fresh mint leaves
3 cups refined sugar
1½ cups vinegar
1 cup water
2 tablespoons of gelatin (2 packets, if using individual portions)
½ cup chopped mint leaves

Directions:
Preheat the oven to 350 degrees. Rub the lamb with olive oil and sprinkle liberal amount of rosemary and salt and pepper to taste all over it. Place the seasoned lamb leg on a rack in a roasting pan. Arrange the potatoes around the lamb and bake for an hour. Remove lamb from the oven, wrap in aluminum foil for ½ hour minutes before carving. Reheat potatoes if needed and serve with mint jelly.

For the mint jelly, combine the fresh mint leaves, sugar, vinegar and water in a non-reactive saucepan. Bring to a boil and simmer for ten minutes. Strain and return to heat. Dissolve the gelatin in ¼ cup of water. Add the dissolved gelatin to the strained mixture, stir and turn off heat. Mix in the chopped mint leaves. Pour into mold (if desired) or into serving dish and refrigerate until gelled. Serve chilled alongside roast lamb and potatoes.

Roast turkey

This is an updated version of roast turkey, using a higher cooking temperature. It is faster and keeps the meat moist.

Ingredients:
1 (15 to 16 pound) frozen young turkey. (This recipe does not work as well for turkeys larger than this.)
Salt and pepper
Aromatics:
1 red apple, sliced
1/2 onion, sliced
1 cinnamon stick
1 cup water
5 sprigs fresh rosemary

5 leaves fresh sage
Canola oil

Directions:
Preheat oven to 500 F.
Place the bird on roasting rack inside a flame-proof roaster and pat dry with paper towels. Season cavity with salt and pepper.

Combine the apple, onion, cinnamon stick, and 1 cup of water in a microwave safe dish and microwave on high for 5 minutes. Add steeped aromatics to the turkey's cavity along with the rosemary and sage. Tuck the wings underneath the bird and coat the skin liberally with canola oil. Season outside of the turkey with salt and pepper.

Roast the turkey on lowest level of the oven at 500 degrees F for 30 minutes. Insert a probe thermometer into thickest part of the breast and reduce the oven temperature to 350 degrees F. A 15 to 16 pound turkey should require a total of 2 to 2 1/2 hours of roasting. Look for a temperature on your meat thermometer of 160 F. Let the turkey rest, loosely covered with foil, for 15 minutes before carving.

Giblet gravy

Serves 12
Ingredients:
1 giblets from a turkey
½ teaspoon salt
½ teaspoon ground black pepper
1 cube chicken bouillon
1 stalk celery, halved
1/4 yellow onion1 quart water

Pan drippings from a roasted turkey poured into a fat separator
4 hard-cooked eggs
2 tablespoons cornstarch
1/2 cup heavy cream
1 tablespoon sweet sherry

Directions:

In a 2-quart saucepan, simmer the giblets, salt, pepper, bouillon, celery and onion in 1 quart of water for 40 to 50 minutes.

Discard celery, onion and gizzard. Chop liver and pull off neck meat without the skin and return to pan. Add turkey drippings. Chop eggs and add to broth. Mix cornstarch and milk together and slowly add to broth. Stir well until thickened. Add sherry. Cover. Reduce heat to low and keep warm.

Turkey Hash

I always looked forward to this use of leftover turkey.

Ingredients:
3 tablespoons margarine
1 large yellow onion, diced
3 cups leftover mashed potatoes
3 cups leftover stuffing
3 cups leftover cooked turkey, diced
1 cup leftover cooked vegetables
Salt and pepper to taste
1/4 cup parsley leaves
1 cup leftover cranberry sauce

Directions:

In a very large iron skillet, melt margarine on medium heat. Add the onion and cook 8 to 10 minutes or until browned, stirring frequently. Stir in mashed potatoes, stuffing, turkey, and vegetables. Cook 20 minutes uncovered, turning occasionally and pressing with spatula, until browned. Season and sprinkle with parsley. Serve with cranberry sauce.

Turkey a la King

Pop served this over toast cut in half diagonally, usually, or canned biscuits prepared according to instructions.

Serves 6.

Ingredients:

3 tablespoons butter or margarine (Pop usually used margarine)

12 ounces fresh mushrooms, sliced

2 tablespoon all-purpose flour

1 ½ cups chicken broth

1 cup heavy cream

2 cups chopped cooked turkey

2/3 cup frozen peas and carrots, thawed

Salt and pepper to taste

Directions:

In a large skillet over medium low heat, cook butter until golden brown. Sauté mushrooms until tender. Stir in flour until smooth. Slowly whisk in chicken broth and cook until slightly thickened. Stir in cream, turkey and peas. Reduce heat to low and cook until thickened. Season with salt and pepper.

Turkey Tetrazzini

This was a family favorite.

Serves 6
Ingredients:
12 ounces spaghetti
2 tablespoons butter or margarine
1 (6 ounce) can sliced mushrooms, drained
1 teaspoon salt
1/4 teaspoon pepper
2 cups chopped cooked turkey
1 (10.75 ounce) can condensed cream of celery soup
1 cup frozen peas and carrots, thawed
1 cup sour cream
1/2 cup grated Parmesan cheese

Directions:
Bring a large pot of lightly salted water to a boil. Add pasta and cook for 8 to 10 minutes or until al dente; drain.

Preheat oven to 375 degrees F

Melt butter in a large heavy skillet. Sauté mushrooms for 1 minute. Season with salt and pepper, and stir in turkey, condensed soup, peas and carrots and sour cream. Place cooked noodles in a large baking dish sprayed with cooking oil. Pour sauce mixture evenly over the top. Sprinkle with Parmesan cheese.

Bake in preheated oven for 20 to 25 minutes, or until sauce is bubbling.

Turkey Casserole

Serves 10. We often had leftovers of this, which was made from leftover turkey. This is about when the bird would be getting a bit tiresome.

Ingredients:

1 (6 ounce) package dry bread stuffing mix
1 can chicken broth
1 (16 ounce) container sour cream
1 (10.75 ounce) can condensed cream of mushroom soup
1 (10.75 ounce) can condensed cream of celery soup
1 (1 ounce) package dry onion soup mix
2 (14.5 ounce) cans cut green beans, drained
2 cups cooked, chopped turkey meat
Salt and pepper to taste

Directions:

Preheat oven to 350 degrees F.

Prepare stuffing according to package directions using chicken broth.

In a medium bowl, mix the sour cream, cream of mushroom soup, cream of celery soup and dry onion soup mix. Season to taste. The soup mix can be salty, so Pop usually only added pepper.

Spread the green beans in a 9x13 inch dish sprayed with cooking oil. Top with a layer of turkey. Pour the soup mixture over the turkey. Top with stuffing.

Bake in the preheated oven 30 minutes, or until browned and bubbly.

Turkey and Rice Soup

Dad would made pick the turkey clean for the other left-over dishes, then prepare the stock for this one ahead of time, freezing the stock until he was ready to finally put the turkey-thon to rest.

Ingredients:

Stock:

1 turkey carcass
1 large onion, halved and skin left on
1 large carrot, roughly chopped
1 stalk celery, roughly chopped
1 head garlic, halved
1 teaspoon dried rosemary
1 teaspoon dried thyme
2 bay leaves
salt and ground black pepper to taste
water to cover

Soup:

2 large onions, diced
2 carrots, diced
2 stalks celery, diced
2 cloves garlic, minced
1 teaspoon poultry seasoning
1 teaspoon dried rosemary
1 teaspoon onion powder

2 cups cooked rice

Directions:

Combine turkey carcass, halved onion, roughly chopped carrot, roughly chopped celery, halved garlic head, 1 teaspoon rosemary, thyme, bay leaves, salt, and pepper in a stockpot; pour in enough water to cover. Bring mixture to a boil, cover pot, reduce heat, and simmer until flavors have blended, about 1 hour.

Years later, a few days after Thanksgiving, I was preparing to lower the carcass into the water before adding the vegetables when my new bride came into the kitchen. "What are you doing?" She shook her head to try to understand what I was up to.

"I'm making the stock for the turkey and rice soup." I figured it was obvious. Didn't everyone eat on the turkey for at least a week or a week and a half?

"Let it go, honey." She patted my arm gently. "It's been a good turkey. We enjoyed it, but it's time to let it go."

I realized that I was being exactly like my father, which isn't a bad thing, but it turns out, I did not live through the Great Depression. We did not have to eat on the poor beast until Christmas. I had to laugh. I threw the pitiful carcass away.

Remove turkey carcass and pull remaining meat from bones; reserve meat and discard carcass. Remove vegetables and bay leaves from stock using a slotted spoon and discard. Skim off any froth from the top of the stock.

Stir diced onions, diced carrots, diced celery, minced garlic, poultry seasoning, 1 teaspoon rosemary, and onion powder into stock; bring to a boil. Reduce heat, cover pot, and simmer until vegetables are very tender, 20 to 30 minutes. Add cooked rice and turkey meat to soup; season with salt and pepper. Cook until rice and turkey meat are warmed, about 5 minutes.

Creamed Onions

This was always one of my favorites.
Serves 6
Ingredients:
1 ½ cups pearl onions
4 cups water
7 tablespoons butter
7 tablespoons all-purpose flour
3 cups heavy cream
salt to taste
ground black pepper to taste
A few grains of ground cayenne pepper
Paprika

Directions:
Peel onions and drop into boiling water. Cook until tender. Drain, reserving liquid. Set onions aside while you make the sauce.

Melt butter in a saucepan over medium heat. Whisk in flour to make a paste. Mix together cooking water and milk. Add milk mixture slowly to the saucepan, stirring constantly, and cook until thickened. Add salt and pepper to taste. Add cayenne and stir. Add onions, heat through, and transfer to a serving dish. Sprinkle with paprika for color.

Sweet Potato Casserole

This was a later addition to Dad's holiday meal that he picked up from one of his many marriages. Honestly, it always seemed a little out of place with his cooking: too sweet and, perhaps, not as much depth of flavor. But it did become a staple.

Serves 6
Ingredients:
1 (29-ounce can) cooked sweet potatoes
1/4 cup brown sugar, packed
2 tablespoons maple syrup
3 tablespoons butter, softened
1 teaspoon salt
1 teaspoon ground cinnamon
½ teaspoon ground nutmeg
1/2 teaspoon vanilla extract
1/2 cup finely chopped pecans, divided
1 cup marshmallows

Instructions:
Heat oven to 375 degrees F. Spray a 11 x 7-inch baking dish with cooking oil spray.

Place potatoes into a large mixing bowl. Add brown sugar, butter, salt, cinnamon, nutmeg and vanilla extract. Mash mixture with a potato masher until an even texture throughout. Stir in 1/4 cup of pecans.

Spread potato mixture into an even layer in the prepared baking dish. Sprinkle remaining 1/4 cup of pecans over the mixture. Top with marshmallows.

Bake at 375 F. for 20 minutes or until marshmallows are toasted. Serve warm.

Stuffed Pork Roast with Port Reduction

Serves 8-10, but the 6 of us rarely had leftovers of this one.

Ingredients:
1 ½ cups tawny port
3/4 cup dried cherries or cranberries, coarsely chopped
2 tablespoons olive oil, divided
¾ cup finely chopped celery
½ cup finely chopped sweet onion
2 large garlic cloves, minced
1 cup breadcrumbs, preferably Panko
2 tablespoons butter, divided
2½ cups chicken stock, divided
1 teaspoon dried sage, divided
½ teaspoon dried thyme
1½ teaspoons kosher salt, divided
1¼ teaspoons freshly ground black pepper, divided
1 (3-pound) pork tenderloin, trimmed
1 shallot, peeled and quartered
1 tablespoon all-purpose flour
1 tablespoon butter, softened

Instructions:
Preheat oven to 400° F.

189

Combine port and cherries/cranberries in a small sauce-pan over medium heat; bring to a boil. Reduce heat; simmer 4 minutes. Remove from heat; let stand 10 minutes. Drain fruit in a sieve over a bowl, reserving fruit and port.

Heat a medium skillet over medium heat. Add 1 table-spoon oil to pan; swirl to coat. Add celery and onion; cook 10 minutes or until vegetables are almost tender, stirring occasion-ally. Add garlic; cook 1 minute, stirring frequently. Combine celery mixture, cherries, and breadcrumbs in a large bowl. Melt 1 tablespoon butter. Drizzle the melted butter and ¼ cup stock over bread mixture, and toss. Stir in half of the sage, thyme, ¼ teaspoon salt, and ¼ teaspoon pepper.

Cut horizontally through center of pork, cutting to, but not through, other side using a sharp knife; open flat, as you would a book. Place pork between 2 large sheets of plastic wrap; pound to an even ½-inch thickness using a meat mallet. Brush 1½ teaspoons oil over inside of pork; sprinkle with ¼ teaspoon salt and ¼ teaspoon pepper. Spread breadcrumb mixture evenly over pork, leaving a ½-inch border around outside edges. Roll up pork, jelly-roll fashion, starting with short side. Secure at 2-inch intervals with twine. Brush outside of pork with remain-ing 1½ teaspoons oil; sprinkle all sides of pork evenly with ¾ teaspoon salt and ½ teaspoon pepper.

Heat a large skillet over high heat. Add pork to pan; cook 8 minutes, turning to brown on all sides. Place pork on a roast-ing rack coated with cooking spray; place rack in a roasting pan. Pour remaining 2¼ cups stock in bottom of roasting pan. Roast pork at 400° for 20-25 minutes or until a thermometer inserted in center of pork registers 138°. Remove pork from pan; let stand 15 minutes. Cut crosswise into 12 slices.

Place roasting pan over medium-high heat; add reserved port and shallot; bring to a boil. Cook until liquid is reduced to 1 cup (about 10 minutes). Combine flour and 1 tablespoon butter and knead into a ball. Add flour mixture to port mixture, stirring to dissolve the flour ball; cook 5 minutes or until port mixture begins to thicken. Strain sauce; discard solids. Stir in remaining remaining sage, ¼ teaspoon salt, and ¼ teaspoon pepper. Serve sauce with pork.

We Got Wheels

In 1969, Neil Armstrong took one small step and changed the world. That same year, The Beatles played their last live concert on the roof of Apple Records. Meanwhile, in upstate New York, half a million young people got together for three days of peace and music. Bell-bottomed jeans and tie-dyed tee-shirts became the fashion trend in 1969 and Midnight Cowboy released that year. The Viet Nam War raged on our televisions through the nightly news each evening. But more important than any of those events for me was, I got my driver's license. Yes, all of those things were the news of the day, and I remember watching them unfold in the newspaper and on the television, our once insulated world changing with each newscast and every passing day, but I had looked forward to getting my driver's license intensely. Our town was built around automobiles. When we were younger, we took the bus or rode bikes, but once we were teens, we were all about cars. Getting to drive meant being set loose, with all that that might portend.

I was a sophomore in high school, which meant at that time my first year at Owensboro High School. My friends and I were the newbies at school, finding our way around the much larger school, piled into a much larger group of all the rising 10th graders from the junior high schools across the city. Everything was changed. I was changed. In fact, I had made a very deliberate choice to not be the same. Despite my classmates encouraging me in my ninth-grade yearbook to "Never Change," I had in fact, decided to make some serious alterations in myself. At the beginning of the summer break, I looked at myself in the bathroom mirror one day and did not like who was looking back at me. I was pudgy. I slouched. Even my face was slack-jawed. I didn't care for this image of myself. Add to that my speech impediment, and I felt a strong desire to redo myself. I believe part of my undertaking this change was a result of losing my brother Bruce in Viet Nam. I had a sense that maybe I didn't have forever, that all lives are limited, including my own. I decided I needed to take some control over myself.

I asked Pop to put up a basketball goal in the driveway, which was very wide and concrete. He did. We measured the height carefully. All summer, I played basketball every day for hours, often straight through lunch. I ran around the driveway and sweated in the hot Kentucky sun. Every shot I took, I practiced saying aloud "Orange" because it was a word I simply could not say correctly before. Dribble, dribble, shoot, "Orange." Chase the ball down (I was never a great shot.). Shoot. "Orange." In the afternoon, I walked the mile and a half to Jimmie's house down Frederica and up 25th to Daviess Street or turning down Booth Avenue and over to Dana's house at Elm Street. The entire walk, I made a point of keeping my back straight. I clenched my jaw to remind myself not to be slack-jawed. And I repeatedly said, "Orange." By the end of the summer, I had lost my chubbiness to the point of being thin. I was even a bit taller, both from natural growth and from now actually standing upright rather than in a Neanderthal slump.

And, I had conquered my speech impediment. My friends who had seen me all summer saw it taking place and so witnessed it gradually, but classmates I had not seen since the previous school year found the change in me striking and a few didn't even recognize me. I learned a great deal about myself that summer, and about how the choices I made could affect my world.

One evening that summer, Dana and I were walking from his house to my house down Frederica. Dana had a paper route and was forever buying odd things, including every copy of his long-standing love affair with Mad Magazine. But this day, he had something extra cool to show. We passed in front of the brick and concrete sign for the college. Traffic on Frederica was heavy, as it usually was.

"Look what I got today." Dana reached into his pocket and pulled out a long, shiny survival knife. I had seen the handle sticking out of his pocket, but I waited until he wanted to share. He pulled the knife out of its sheath and let the light flint off the metal. "Look at this." He unscrewed the top. "Look." He emptied the contents into his palm as we walked. "Matches. Fishing line. Two hooks. And check this out." He pulled a long thin wire saw from the handle. I had to admit; it was cool. It never really mattered that neither of us as kids in the city might need such a tool; it was just impressive. He stuffed the survival tools back into the handle, replaced the top, and handed the knife to me. We kept walking. We were across the street from the radio station. It was just beginning to turn dusk. I handled the blade with the reverence it deserved, although in fact it was not in the least sharp. Then I had a great idea. Well, no, it was a really bad idea, but I thought it was a great idea.

"Hey, I know." I brandished the knife back and forth. "I'll walk back over here in the field and act like I'm sneaking up on you. You act like your scared and get ready to run, but then I'll act like I'm stabbing you. All the people in the cars will think they saw a murder!" Cars whizzed back and forth next to us.

"Okay." Dana would always partake in my foolish ideas. It should be noted that we usually spurred each other on in often risky endeavors. "That'd be fun!" He shot me his wide grin.

I detoured into the field. Dana approached College Drive as I sneaked up behind him with the knife, which I twisted in my hand so the light would glint from the blade. Dana quickened his step and looked over his shoulder nervously. It grew a bit darker and the streetlights came on. I ran up behind Dana just as he feigned a run and acted like I was stabbing him in the gut. He doubled over like a stuntman, falling to the sidewalk just as two cars ran up over the curb and onto the sidewalk and a police car screeched to a halt on College Drive, his lights on and siren blaring. I took off running and Dana, still clutching his not-stabbed belly, yelled, "Run, Larry. They got me." And they did have him. Concerned drivers had run to his rescue and were even now trying to administer to his knife wound which he most certainly did not have. I ran across the yard of the big brick church, tossing Dana's prized knife into the bushes. The policeman had exited his car and ran after me. I made it to Standish Place North, about a block and a half when the cop picked me up by my collar, my legs still churning. I heard a guy behind him call, "Got the knife." I stopped struggling and the cop put me down.

"I didn't stab him. Honest. We were just playing."

"Uh huh." He looked over and saw Dana standing now, obviously unhurt. "What the hell were you doing?" He shook his head.

"Um, um." I stared wide-eyed. His interrogation technique was brutal – he stared hard at me with a face of disapproval.

"Trying to fool the cars?" He looked at me knowingly now.

I paused. There was no denying it. "Yes sir." I looked at the ground.

Another man came up leading Dana by the arm. "Here's the other one." Dana and I shot each other a look. We had no clue we would be so successful in our ruse. Jail awaited. Perhaps hard time, breaking rocks in our striped uniforms, chains around our ankles.

"I got it. Thanks." The policeman half turned and the man handed the policeman the wonderful survivalist knife, with none of Dana's blood dripping from the blade. The policeman looked at us both and suppressed a bit of a smirk as he shook his head. The other man walked away. "Whose is this?" I didn't say anything. If ownership equaled blame, I didn't want to turn in Dana. The policeman inspected the knife.

"It's mine." Dana hung his head.

The policeman handed it to him. "It's cool. Try not to be stupid with it, okay?" Dana and I looked up at each other. I promise you, I had fully expected a paddy wagon to pull up, for us to be tossed in unceremoniously, and for the next scene to be calling our parents for bail money, which may or may not have been forthcoming. "Where you heading?"

"My house." I jerked my thumb towards our house which was clearly visible. Pop's Buick was in the driveway. "It's right there. My Dad's home."

"Don't get into any more trouble, okay?" The policeman looked around to see if anyone were still around, but everyone else had left. "Go home." He shook his head and walked away. Dana and I barely spoke the remaining block or so across the vacant lots.

When we sat down to dinner to Dad's corned beef and cabbage, Dad asked us what was going on, but we did not confess our mock murder, we simply murmured, "Nothin'," as we shot glances across the table at each other.

If I was a new me starting at OHS, I was still just a sophomore, one of the babies of the school. The seniors seemed like giants compared to us, although since Ernie was, in fact, a senior, I had some immediate credibility. It also meant I carried some of his notoriety. Ernie's teen years are one for an entirely different book. To say he was a hellion does the term something of an injustice. Tales of Ernie's misdeeds live on in the lore of an entire generation of Owensboroans. To be honest, I had my own share of misadventures, but, for one thing, I usually tried not to get caught. Ernie usually committed his transgressions in the face of authority. But I never was quite as mischievous overall as Ernie. He had a reputation of being a rowdy kid, despite being small in stature. That he gathered around him not only good, long-term friends, but also some of the biggest bullies in town meant anyone my age was in awe of Ernie and his crazy behavior.

At that time at Owensboro High School, every boy had to take at least one semester of ROTC. Of course, this was during The Viet Nam War and the idea of taking ROTC was anathema to just about all of us. Ernie took it every semester. Not because he wanted to be a soldier, or that he even wanted to be in ROTC. He took it every semester because he was thrown out of the class every time he took it and had to have a credit to graduate. The last time he was thrown out was for setting the giant trash bin on fire and nearly burning down the ROTC building. He never did complete the class and eventually was invited to complete his high school experience at any school that was not OHS. But very few of us wanted to be in ROTC, so he was not alone in that.

My first day at OHS in ROTC, the teacher, a sergeant, called roll. "Troutman?"

"Here."

"Walters?"

"Here."

"Wardrip?"

"Here."

"Weill?"

I raised my hand, somewhat defiantly I thought. My desire to disobey The Man was not yet strong. "Here." My voice croaked.

"Wait." Sarge looked up at me over his half-glasses. "Weill?"

"Yes sir?" I thought of what trouble I could possibly be in before class had even begun.

"You any relation to Bruce Weill? Ernie Weill?" He took his glasses off now and looked hard at me. I can still see his flat-top.

"Yeah, they're my brothers." My hackles were raised a bit. Not yet a full-blown hippie, I was at least protective of family.

"See me after class." Sarge went back to the roster. "Whitmer?"

"Here."

I stayed after class, my defenses on alert. I went up to the desk. "You wanted to see me?"

Sarge took off his glasses again and looked at me. He lay his arms across the desk, almost pleading. "Look. I don't want any more trouble, okay? Just don't come, okay? Read the book. Take the tests. Show up for inspection. Otherwise, just don't come." He shook his head and went back to his gradebook.

"Yes sir!" I left almost giddy. Thanks, brothers!

I did read the book, a dated crumpled army edition eloquently titled ROTCM 145-4-1. I learned to disassemble, clean and reassemble an M-1 rifle. I learned how to polish brass buttons on my heavy woolen army surplus uniform. And I let my hair grow longer and longer.

I read the army manual enough to pass the class and be done with it. But I studied the driver's license manual more carefully than I had studied any book in my life. I knew all the shapes of various street signs and what they meant. I learned when to use a turn signal and how to use hand signals if the car did not have lighted signals. (Okay, this was a while back.) I even memorized how many feet I was supposed to leave between the car in front of me and my car, depending on speed. Nowadays, the training manuals talk about time between cars, but back then, it was feet. I passed the written test, although I was quite nervous, then learned to drive in Pop's boat, I mean, Buick Electra 225. It was an awesome car and absolutely huge. It had power everything and was very easy to drive. I was ready. I parallel parked and learned to turn around by backing into an alley and pulling out. I passed my driver's test and was duly armed. I was free to go forth and be free to the wind.

The only problem with my newfound freedom was, I had a driver's license, but I had no car. Dad sometimes let me use his car on Friday or Saturday night, but often, he was using it himself. Some of my friends had cars and we rode around together after school and sometimes on weekends, but it wasn't the same. I was still isolated. One Saturday, I called each of my friends to see what was going on, but they were all out already. I was frustrated. But the irony was, there was a car in the driveway. And the key was in the kitchen drawer. No one else was home, so I could surely use the car, except that it was a manual transmission and I had never driven a four-speed. As I sat, bored and alone, I decided that since I had seen Ernie drive it, I could figure it out. I knew the concept. I could do this. So I went out and climbed into the maroon 1964 Corvair in the drive and proceeded to teach myself how to drive it. I started it up, foot on the clutch, put it in reverse, let go of the clutch and did a backwards donut into the field next to the house and the engine died. Fortunately, no one had been passing by on Halifax Drive to be t-boned at that particular moment. I realized I had let go of the clutch too quickly. I started it back up, released the clutch more slowly and did about five serious lurches. I pushed in the clutch again and stopped the car. I caught my breath, gave it some gas, slowly released the clutch and drove off down Standish Place. I still had a few hiccups, but from that point on, that Corvair was mine. It had been Ernie's, but he now had a muscle car, an Olds 442 that was just silly in its power. But it was cool. But I was elated with the Corvair. It was by the standards of the day, on the small side, but it was larger on the inside than many SUVs of today. It was an air-cooled, rear engine vehicle, two-door with folding front seats. The trunk was in the front of the car and was simply a rubber lined box with a plug in the bottom should water get in. That the trunk could serve as a wonderful cooler was not lost on me and my pals.

When I got home that day from driving to my friends' houses and cruising through the drive-through restaurant, Pop had gotten home and was doing the prep work for having beef and kidney pie for supper the next day, which meant Rhoda was staying at Chessie's since there was zero possibility of her eating kidney. I came bopping in, quite proud of myself. Dad looked up from the sink.

"Where have you been?" He sliced open a kidney and pulled off a fatty tendon.

"Just driving." I beamed a little, I think.

"In the Corvair?" He rinsed the kidneys off and put them into a bowl of water to soak. He tossed in a palm full of salt.

"Yes sir." I watched him walk over to the refrigerator and put the bowl in.

"Since when do you drive a four-speed?" Pop closed the fridge, wiped his hands on a dish towel and removed his apron.

"Well, since today, I guess."

"Ernie teach you?" Pop walked over to his favorite leather sling chair and sat down, pulling his Winstons from his shirt pocket.

"Ernie's not here. I taught myself."

Pop looked up at me. "Taught yourself, huh?" He smiled.

"Yes sir." I went over to counter drawer and dropped the key in.

"No, you keep the key. If you can drive it, you keep the key." He pulled smoke from his cigarette and tapped the ashes off into the heavy glass hexagonal ashtray he had had forever, even after it had gotten a small chip in it. I put the key in my pocket and bounced back to my room. I had wheels! I was ecstatic. I lay on my bed listening to Sly and the Family Stone and feeling free in a way I had not felt before. I had wheels!

Having a car meant everything was open for me now. I drove myself to school each morning, parking in the muddy vacant lot across Ford Avenue from the school. The school board had purchased the parcel for kids to park in, but it was never paved nor even graveled. But I didn't care. I was driving. It was a little disconcerting, however, that if I had to ford any of the frequent mud puddles, the brakes on the Corvair would not work until they dried out. I guess it made me a more artful puddle dodger though. And after school, I could proceed the four blocks down Frederica, past the giant sassafras tree, to cruise through The Dairy Drive-In, or the "DDI" as we all called it. It was the place to see and be seen by everyone. Or at least you would be seen by everyone at OHS. The students from Owensboro Catholic High usually went to The Dipper on Parish Avenue and the kids from Daviess County went to Wyndalls Wonder Whip, although those were not hard and fast rules. I don't recall anyone being excluded in particular, it was just where each group of kids knew their classmates would be. The DDI itself faced Frederica and sometimes we went that way, pulling into the drive from Frederica and around back to the parking area that had the wavy metal awning above and small scratchy-sounding speakers affixed to the supports where we ordered French fries and Cokes and the occasional hamburger. The food was brought to our cars by a wiry fellow who seemed to despise the job, but I'm sure we were never good tippers. More often than pulling through the parking lot, we turned down Washington Street just before the restaurant then cruised through the alleyway behind the DDI where all the cars faced once they stopped for a snack. We stopped and chatted, looked to see who was in whose car since having a girl in your car at the DDI was tantamount to going steady. If a spot was open, we would back into the opening since facing the alleyway was required by the social etiquette of the times. If we were just with our pals, we would be three, four, five to a car, cruising through, then turning on the access road behind the shopping center. After school, the parking spaces filled up quickly, so getting a front row spot was difficult. So usually, we just cruised through, then went south out Frederica Street to the edge of town (actually about to our house on Halifax), then turned around and drove north to the Ohio River, turned around, drove south, detouring through the DDI, rinse, lather, repeat. I usually had a couple of my best friends with me: Jimmie, George, Sam, Henry, and Mark. I took girls too, but everyone knew being seen at the DDI with a girl meant you were serious, so unless she was my steady girl, we avoided being seen there.

Then we would head to our homes for the evening. When I got home, I would often snack on salted herring that Pop had gotten to soak in milk then cook, but I usually ate it straight from the package. I was a pretty typical teenage boy, so eating that snack would not discourage my appetite for dinner, since it would be delicious even if it was easy, like one of Pop's week night favorites, sausage patties and baked apples.

Having a driver's license meant going on dates now in a new way. No longer required to be picked up and brought home by parents left us on our own to find things to do and places to go. We sometimes went downtown to the movie house and there was a newer movie house in Wesleyan Park Plaza we frequented. Easy Rider, Butch Cassidy and the Sundance Kid, The Prime of Miss Jean Brodie were all popular. There were James Bond movies and a slew of spaghetti westerns. I would pick up my date, drive out to Cornell's or, if it was a special occasion, Gabe's. Then we went to the movies often, sometimes indoors, but more often at The Cardinal Drive-in or The Starlight Drive-in, where we would watch the movies, munch popcorn, and kiss. We drove to concerts at the Armory and the Sports Center and even over to Evansville for big name concerts at Roberts Arena, although we saw some very good acts in our own hometown, from Fleetwood Mac to The Byrds to Paul Revere and the Raiders. We went to football and basketball games, and school dances. We were carefree, although the travails of teen dating seemed much larger than they truly were, but that was more testament to our naïveté than anything else.

But being 16 and driving also meant we were left on our own much more. Rhoda was twelve and didn't need the babysitting she once did, although Chessie was still a frequent visitor. But most days, we were on our own all afternoon. We of course did not always use our freedom responsibly. We skipped class at lunch to drive down to The Eight Ball to play pinball, shoot pool, and eat a Big Jess hamburger. I can still see Jess, his apron covered in grease, slamming a beef ball onto the grill with such force, it was immediately transformed from beef ball to beef patty, and a thin one at that. It also added to the layer of grease on his apron. We played eight ball usually, a quarter a game which was paid by calling over the young man with the rack, who filled the rack and took your payment. If you tipped him, which we usually did, albeit not a lot, he would listen for you to call him again, and you could call him back for the next set-up by saying "rack" in an everyday sort of level and he heard it over the din of the pool hall. We would lag for break, and then, usually, I would lose a game of pool. I was never any good at it. Lucky for me, I recognized that inability early on so never wagered on my games.

On weekends, several of us would climb into my friend Rowe's Volkswagon and drive out into the country, drinking beer. I met Rowe through my buddy Jimmie and his cousin. I found Rowe funny, witty, smart, and a little crazy. We would be four in the car and we would split a six pack of tallboys, which were 16-ounce cans of beer. We would drive as fast as a VW Beetle could go out Miller's Mill Road, turn onto Deserter Creek Road and head out to the tiny crossroad of Taffy, Kentucky. Then we would turn around and come back, drinking beer, feeling invincible as only teenaged boys can feel and driving fast. Deserter Creek was so named because it had only occasionally actually running water. Most of the time, it was little more than a dry ditch. But one rainy spring afternoon, as we barreled along Deserter Creek Road, we crested a hill and found to our dismay that the creek had returned, and in full vigor. The road was completely submerged. Rowe had no opportunity to stop or even swerve, so we headed straight into the creek. I should say, we went onto the creek since we were moving fast enough and were in a Beetle so that we actually skimmed across the top of the creek and landed on the opposite bank. We were not on the road and were mired in mud, but we were alive, so we considered ourselves extremely lucky. We pushed the car out and made it home, laughing nervously about our adventure, but we kept seeing that expanse of water in the windshield headed towards us. We avoided that route on rainy days thereafter.

Having the freedom a car afforded us brought new opportunities but also new responsibilities. We embraced the opportunities more than the obligations, of course, but that was a part of growing up in those times. We were stretching our wings, making the same mistakes made by teenagers for generations, and learning who we were. It was the awkward time between too young to know better and too full of bravado to resist the challenge.

Beef and kidney pie

Ingredients:
1 refrigerated pie pastry for a 9-inch pie
1 pound beef kidney
2 pounds bottom round steak, cut into 1 ½ inch cubes
2 tablespoons shortening
2 yellow onions, chopped coarsely
2 teaspoons Kosher salt
1/2 teaspoon ground black pepper
        1/2 teaspoon dried thyme
1 bay leaf
1 tablespoon Worcestershire sauce
2 cups water

4 cups diced russet potatoes
1 cup diced carrots
6 tablespoons all-purpose flour

Directions:

Remove fatty tendon and tubes from kidney and cover with lightly salted water. Cover tightly and refrigerate overnight. Drain thoroughly and dice.

In a Dutch oven, brown kidney and steak in hot shortening over medium heat. Add onions, seasonings, and 1 1/2 cups water. Lower temperature to medium low and simmer until meat is almost tender, about 1 hour. Add potatoes and carrots and continue simmering until vegetables are tender, around 1/2 hour.

Blend together flour and remaining 1/2 cup water; stir into meat mixture. Continue cooking and stirring until mixture thickens. Remove the pot from the stove and allow to cool while you roll out pastry the pastry dough slightly larger than top of Dutch oven. Place the pie crust over meat mixture, and trim to overhang 1 inch. Fold under, and flute against inside edge of pot. Cut several steam vents in center.

Bake at 425 degrees until browned, about 30 minutes.

Salted Herring

I often ate this as it was from the package. It's a strong flavor, to be sure.

Serves four as an appetizer.

Ingredients:

1 ½ pounds smoked herring. Dad bought it in filets.
2 cups milk
2 tablespoons plus ¼ cup extra-virgin olive oil

Chopped fresh parsley
1 lemon, cut into wedges
Ground black pepper to taste
Saltine crackers

Instructions:

Place the herring in a long ceramic or glass baking pan and cover with milk. Cover with plastic wrap and place in the refrigerator, covered, for at least 5 hours, turning occasionally. Remove the fish from the refrigerator, rinse and dry thoroughly.

Heat 2 tablespoons oil in a large heavy skillet. Place the herring in the pan and cook, turning once, until golden in color, about 5-6 minutes on each side. Cut into cracker sized pieces and arrange on a serving platter, pour the olive oil over, sprinkle with the parsley and season with pepper. Serve with lemons and saltine crackers.

Baked apples

In many families, this is a dessert, but Pop served this as a side dish to fried sausage patties that were 1/3 pound each
Serves 6
Ingredients:
6 large Winesap apples, peeled and cored
3 tablespoons butter
3 tablespoons brown sugar
1 ½ teaspoon ground cinnamon
Allspice to taste

Directions:

Preheat over to 375 degrees. Arrange apples in a greased two quart baking dish. Fill each apple center with ½ tablespoon butter, ½ tablespoon brown sugar, ¼ teaspoon gound cinnamon and a sprinkle of allspice. Fill with water up to a quarter of the height of the apples. Bake for one hour.

Corned beef and Cabbage

Serves 8
Ingredients:
1 (3-4 pound) corned beef brisket with spice packet
10-12 small red potatoes, halved
6 medium carrots, peeled and cut into 3" pieces
1 medium head cabbage, cut into wedges
Horseradish Mustard Sauce:
1 cup sour cream
2 tablespoons Dijon mustard
1/4 teaspoon sugar
1 ½ tablespoons prepared creamy horseradish

Directions:
Place brisket and contents of seasoning packet in a large Dutch oven or stockpot and cover with water. Bring to a boil. Reduce heat; simmer, covered, 2 ½ hours.

Add potatoes and carrots, cover, and return to a boil. Reduce heat and simmer until vegetables are tender, 30-40 minutes. Add cabbage to pot; return to a boil. Reduce heat; simmer, covered, until cabbage is tender, about 15 minutes. Remove brisket from the water and let it drain a little, then slice across the grain and serve with the vegetables. Serve the sauce on the side.

Horseradish Mustard Sauce: Mix all ingredients well and refrigerate for 30 minutes.

Boston Baked Beans

Serves 6
Ingredients:
1 pound dry navy beans or great northern
6 cups water
Pinch of baking soda
1 bay leaf
6 strips thick sliced bacon, cut in 1/2-inch pieces
1 medium yellow onion, diced
1/3 cup molasses
1/4 cup packed dark brown sugar
1 ½ teaspoon dry mustard
1 ½ teaspoon salt, or to taste
1 teaspoon freshly ground black pepper

Directions:
Soak the beans in the 6 cups of water overnight in a large saucepan or Dutch oven. Add a pinch of baking soda and bay leaf, and bring to a boil. Reduce the heat to medium and simmer for 15 minutes. Drain into a colander set over a large bowl to reserve the liquid.

Preheat oven to 300 F.

Transfer the drained beans into a Dutch oven and add the rest of the ingredients. Stir until combined. Add enough of the reserved water to just barely cover the beans. Cover the pot tightly and place in the oven for 1 hour.

Uncover and check the liquid level - do not stir. Add some reserved liquid if the beans are getting too dry. Cover and cook 1 more hour. Uncover again and test the beans; they should be getting tender, but if they're still firm, cover and cook a bit longer, adding a splash of water if needed.

When the beans are tender, turn the heat up to 350 F and continue to cook uncovered for another 30 minutes or so. This last 30 minutes is to give the beans a nice crust on top, as well as reduce the liquid to a thick, syrupy consistency. Remove when ready and serve hot or room temperature.

Cabbage and Apples

This was a dish the Dad said was inherited from his German grandmother.

Serves 6-8
Ingredients:
1 large head cabbage, 2 to 2 1/2 pounds, quartered, cored and cut crosswise in thin strips
2 tablespoons vegetable oil
1 small white onion, thinly sliced
2 granny smith apples, peeled, cored and sliced
About 1/3 cup cider vinegar
¼ teaspoon ground allspice
Salt
Freshly ground pepper to taste

Directions:
Prepare the cabbage, and cover with cold water while you prepare the remaining ingredients.
Heat the oil over medium heat in a large, lidded skillet or casserole, and add the onion. Cook, stirring, until just about tender, about three minutes. Add 2 tablespoons of the vinegar

and cook, stirring, until the mixture is golden, about three minutes, then add the apples and stir for two to three minutes.

Drain the cabbage and add to the pot. Toss to coat thoroughly, then stir in the allspice, another 2 tablespoons vinegar, and salt to taste. Toss together. Cover the pot, and cook over low heat for one hour, stirring occasionally. Add freshly ground pepper, taste and adjust salt, and add another tablespoon or two of vinegar as desired.

Trouble

Like most teenagers, I took too many risks and tempted fate far too often as a young man, but I managed to live and, on the whole, through a combination of deviousness and luck, did not suffer nearly as much grief as I probably deserved or that I am sure I caused. My boyhood friends and I have recounted many times we perhaps had no right to expect to have survived and while we certainly got in trouble, we really could have gotten in much more than we did. Still, we had our moments.

It was the summer of 1970. There were four of us boys tooling around town aimlessly one Thursday afternoon, looking for something to do. It was Kentucky July hot and we were out of school and bored. It was a bad recipe. We debated our options. Perhaps we could call on various friends to see if they had any exciting plans. It was an unlikely prospect in the middle of a scorching day in the middle of the week, but at least worth considering. Then again at that time calling on our friends meant driving over to their houses with no guarantee of their being home, or going to one of our own homes to make phone calls. We weren't close to any of our houses so that was perhaps more trouble than it was worth. We could use some dimes in a pay phone somewhere to call out some pals, but it suddenly seemed like too much work with little chance of a payoff. Maybe we should go back to the Dairy Drive In, or the DDI, as we called it. But we had already been there, sitting in the hot car for an hour next to the backlit plastic menu and two-way intercom, watching the occasional friends and acquaintances cruise through the alleyway. True, it was the place to go if you went to the city school to be seen and to see who was around. We had been there, nursed along some colas, and split an order of French fries. We had clowned around, given each other good-natured if sometimes rough ribbing, and waited for people we knew to drive through, but it had been too quiet, so we left. Going back was no good. Then someone had the idea of going out to the abandoned strip mines outside town to go swimming. This was an option we immediately liked. It was definitely hot enough and it would give us something to do, at the very least, and besides, there was a good chance some girls might be out there too, sunbathing and swimming. And even if they weren't, we would have fun by ourselves, daring each other to jump off the cliffs (one of those times we tempted fate with our lives) and cutting up.

We seized on the plan. This was it! Something fun to do on a searing July afternoon. But then we hit a snag: we simply couldn't go to the strip pits the way we were; that is, without beer. It's true we weren't especially dressed for a swim, with only shorts and cut-off jeans, and we had no towels or anything, but those details would never have stopped us. But going all the way out to the secret teen hangout in West Louisville without at least a little beer would be very un-cool. We weighed our options as we turned onto Breckinridge Street, heading aimlessly for downtown in Mark's '57 Chevy. Ricky had shotgun, Jimmie and I were in the backseat, the windows rolled down so the sultry summer air at least blew across us, mussing our shaggy haircuts. The heat was stifling.

"We gotta have some beer before we head out. Where can we get some beer?" Ricky leaned back in the seat, twisting his head to talk to us in the back. We were only seventeen, far too young be drinking, much less buying alcohol, but we had a plan and we wouldn't let it go, so we strategized how to get beer. "Hey, Larry, can your brother get us some? Is he twenty-one yet?"

"Nah, he's only nineteen. Besides, he's working today, and he wouldn't do it anyway."

"What about Johnny James?" Jimmie asked. Johnny James was the biggest kid in school, and the school bootlegger and bully. "He charges too much, but he can always get it."

"Nah, that's no good. Last time we used him, he claimed he got caught. Kept all our money. I don't trust him."

"Dutchman's." Mark said matter-of-factly. He turned on his signal to head up Fourth Street. It was true Dutchman's had a reputation of selling pretty loosely to folks of questionable age, although I had never tested it. This was long before mandatory identification checks. Still, an ID did help and as far as I knew, none of us had one.

"How're you gonna do that? You got an ID, Mark?" Jimmie's horn-rimmed glasses reflected the sun-light. If Mark now had a fake ID, there were lots of untold possibilities for trouble in our future.

"Don't need one." Mark pressed on the gas after the light changed and we rolled up Fourth. There wasn't much up here, just railroad tracks leading to the grain mill, a couple of smoky barbeque spots, then after that the old power plant.

"You don't?" I was dubious. "How're you gonna get beer with no ID?"

"Nah," Ricky chimed in. "Mark's right. Dutchman's will sell to us. Heck, they'll sell to anyone. I'm in. Who else is in?"

"I'm in."

"Me too."

"Who has any money?" I reached into the pocket of my cut-offs. "I've got two and a half dollars." I counted out my coins. It was a perennial problem for teens: too much time and not enough money. All of us had summer jobs, low-paying service positions cleaning buildings at night or manning the boat dock on the river on weekends or the like, but the funds we received we generally used up over the weekend taking our girlfriends out.

"And I'm almost out of gas, so we'll need some gas money too." Mark glanced at his dash. I saw Jimmie craning his neck to see if Mark was lying, trying to get us to fill up his tank so he wouldn't have to spend any of his meager paycheck the next day on gas for the behemoth he drove. Jimmie's resigned slump into his seat told me Mark was telling the truth.

"Larry, you're lying. You've got more than that." Jimmie pulled out his wallet. "I've got five. Fork it over."

"No, all I have is two dollars and fifty cents."

"Get a job."

"Hey, I have a . . ."

"I've got four."

"That's enough," Mark wheeled the car around in the parking lot across from the grain mill. It was true. At around $.36 a gallon for gas and beer being around $3.75, $11.50 was plenty.

"What about you, Mark?" I smelled subterfuge.

"It's my car, and I'm the one risking arrest for buying beer." He had an undeniable point.

Ricky twisted around in his seat again. "Jimmie, you and Larry get out and wait here. If we all four going driving up, they'll know we're underage."

"Why don't you get out and I'll take shotgun?" Jimmie hated being ordered around.

"You don't even look seventeen, much less twenty-one. I'm bigger." This time, Ricky was the one who had a good point. Between the two of us, Jimmie and I barely tipped a scale. Mark pulled over into the parking lot of the King Charles's Inn, a local diner and beer establishment that catered to the workers at the granary. The lot was mostly empty, but Jimmie and I walked the opposite direction once we got out of Mark's boat of a car, meandering towards the switching tracks that led into the mill.

"We'll pick you up here in four hours," Ricky called from the window.

"Funny!" We felt the sun on our skin quickly as we watched Mark and Ricky drive off with our meager funds, leaving us pretty much in the middle of nowhere. We ambled up the tracks, taking turns balancing along the tracks before we pushed each other off. We picked up rocks from between the ties and tossed them as far as we could up the tracks. We sat on the warm rails, lay across them as if we were to be run over, and teased each other about whatever girl each was seeing. In short, we hung around like seventeen year olds. We were best friends from grade school and our attitudes were relaxed and easy towards each other. By the time Mark and Ricky returned, we were sweaty and dirty from the horseplay and the heat, but since we were heading out to the strip pits, we didn't care. We would jump in as soon as we got there. The big Chevy rolled to a stop next to us, a cloud of dust surrounding us.

"Get in!" Ricky waved us to the car. We ran over and climbed in to find a six-pack of "tall boys" on the floor board of the back seat. We were set! In fifteen minutes, we would be having some fun at last on a boring, boiling summer day. Mark turned the car around and we headed up Center Street. We grinned at each other, proud of our great skill at problem solving and tickled to have the prospects for an adventure ahead of us, even if it was only heading out for a swim and a cold beer.

"Crap." Mark was looking in his mirror. The other three of us twisted around and saw the blue lights at the same time we heard the "whoop!" of the siren. It was perhaps our worst nightmare: getting caught under age with beer. Where could we hide the beer? The car was huge inside and out, but there was no place to put the six pack. Mark started pulling over.

"Wait, we gotta hide the beer, Mark!" Jimmie was frantic, but it was too late. Mark had pulled to the side and already, a husky policeman was sauntering up to the side of his car, looking directly at the beer, it seemed. We were doomed. There was no escaping huge trouble.

"Afternoon, boys." The policeman stopped at the back window, staring at the beer. "Kinda hot, huh?" He had a lighter tone to his voice than the situation deserved, I thought. He stepped up to Mark's window. "Lemmee see yer license, son." I felt a deep, dark cloud coming over me. I knew I was about to be arrested. What would my Dad do? He was never an overly strict disciplinarian, although there were the rare instances when he had spanked me (all well-deserved, I might point out). But I was maybe too old for a spanking. Would he ground me? We had a house with outside doors in every room, and he worked all day, so enforcement was a problem. But I would have abided by a grounding, since being told to stay home and read all day was not that far out of my normal realm anyway. He might cut off phone privileges. That would be hard on a bored teenager. I figured that would be included in whatever punishment he meted out, but it would no doubt grow beyond that quickly. All these thoughts raced through my head while the policeman checked all of our ID's.

Meanwhile, his partner called a paddy wagon to come pick us up. I was absolutely devastated. A paddy wagon. I was a criminal. My life was surely forfeit now. All my dreams, all my hopes, dashed. I had destroyed my life for probably one beer. And my father was going to ensure I suffered for many weeks to come. What had I done? We slumped in a ragged line against the back of Mark's Chevy now, mindful of the stares from anyone who happened to pass by. Then the paddy wagon arrived, siren blaring, lights flashing. You'd have thought they had caught Bugs Moran.

"Climb in, boys." The arresting officer opened the back of the van and we piled in morosely. Once we were in, he got in the front passenger seat to take us down. He turned and looked through the metal screen at us. "It's a hot day, boys. I know a cold beer sounds good, but you gotta be twenty-one." He grinned at us, although not maliciously.

"How'd you know?" Mark asked. "How'd you know we had beer?"

"Those two hanging around the rail yard, cutting up." He motioned towards Jimmie and me. "It was clear you were up to something."

"Thanks a lot," Ricky mumbled at us.

"I think it was your idea, Ricky."

"Whatever."

At the police station, they did the whole process, finger printing, photos, the works. I wasn't sure what options I now had for my future as a "con." They put us in a room with mirrors on one wall, just like the television shows, but they didn't bother questioning us. They had all they needed, and besides, as juveniles, we were guilty until proven innocent, which we were not. One by one, we were released to our parents until I was alone in the dungeon – okay, squad room. I continued to mull over my punishments Dad would be meting out. Beatings, groundings, isolation, lectures, yelling – so many options and I could not bring myself to believe any of them would be more than I deserved. Then, Dad showed up.

His face was stone, unmoved, without emotion. He came in with the same officer who arrested us who motioned towards me. "He's all yours." Dad didn't speak. He didn't even look at me. He turned and walked out of the room and I stood frozen, not knowing what to do for a moment until the policeman waved for me to follow Dad. I ran down the hallway to catch up. He still did not speak. I wondered what I should say. There was no way to lie my way out; that much I knew. I bit my lip and followed Dad down Allen Street to his car, parked in front of the Kenyon Apartments. We drove home in silence. Any number of times, I started to speak up, to say how sorry I was for getting in trouble, for doing something that put me in this spot, for breaking the law. But nothing seemed appropriate and Dad was stolidly quiet. When we finally pulled into the driveway at home, he pushed the Elektra into park and finally turned to me and spoke. His face showed no emotion, except maybe a slight expression of resignation.

"I am so disappointed in you."

He turned and exited the car and I sat there, crushed. It was the hardest thing I had ever had to hear. I was a disappointment. I had failed my father. He could not have punished me more if he had beaten me. In fact, I would have preferred all the other punishments I had imagined over his simple honest expression of disappointment in me, and not just my behavior – in me as a son, as a human being. And the fact that I knew I had earned it made it all the more painful. I slinked into my room and flopped on my bed, wondering if there would ever to be a way for me to renew my father's pride in me.

Interestingly, Dad never really said much more about it. I received no other punishment from him, and the juvenile court judge, who was the father of one of my best friends, was always fairly benevolent unless you made return visits to his court, so all I got was a stern warning and a notation in some file somewhere. The only other comment my Dad made was the night of my arrest as we sat at the dinner table, Dad's ham steak, a bubbling baking dish full of scalloped potatoes and a huge salad spread before us. As we sat, he gave me a withering glance, then took his seat. I sat and, being deep into my self-pity, slumped back in my chair.

"Sit up." He folded his hands to say grace.

"Yes sir. I'm sorry."

"You sure as hell are." Then he recited the blessing.

Baked Ham Steaks

Serves 6
Ingredients:
2 center cut ready to eat ham steaks
1/2 cup brown sugar, packed
2 tablespoons prepared mustard
½ teaspoon ground cloves

Directions:
Preheat oven to 375 degrees
Place ham in shallow pan.
Combine mustard with brown sugar and cloves; spread over ham.
Bake ham for twenty minutes

Au Gratin Potatoes

Serves 6
Ingredients:
3 tablespoons butter
3 tablespoons all-purpose flour
1-1/2 teaspoons salt
1/8 teaspoon pepper
2 cups milk
Dash Worcestershire
1 cup shredded cheddar cheese
6 sliced peeled russet potatoes
1/2 medium yellow onion, chopped

Directions:
Preheat oven to 375°. In a large saucepan, melt butter over low heat. Stir in flour, salt and pepper until smooth and cook for 1 minute. Gradually add milk. Add Worcestershire. Bring to a boil; cook and stir until thickened, about two minutes. Remove from heat; stir in cheese until melted. Add potatoes and onion.

Transfer to an oiled 2-qt. baking dish. Cover and bake 45 minutes. Uncover; bake 25-30 minutes or until the potatoes are tender.

Old enough to know better

Being a teenager is not always easy. Sure, those years can be full of carefree days, much more carefree than teenagers perhaps realize, usually, since a part of being a teenager is you believe things in your life are far more important than they actually are. As a result, high school dating, making friends, and fitting in become over-emphasized. And all of that going on while kids' bodies are changing and sending weird new chemicals through them. It's all part of learning to be an adult. And we did have fun. I still have friends that I made in those days, and I am glad for the lessons I learned, although it was striking to look back even a few months after graduation from high school and realize how unimportant many of the events that I took so seriously turned out to be in the bigger picture.

Being old enough to care for ourselves meant being left to our own devices far more often. This was especially true on weekends in the summer, when my younger sister went to our grandmother's apartment to stay the weekend and to walk downtown to either the J. J. Newberry or S.S. Kresge department store. (It's odd to me now that we had to have their initials – why was that?) There, at the lunch counter of one store, then later on when Chessie's (our grandmother) friend Juanita changed jobs, at the other, my sister would be treated to an egg sandwich. Rhoda and Chessie spent the weekends playing board games, reading books, and listening to Chessie's albums of showtunes and, occasionally, Mario Lanza. I can recall the covers of the record sets: Oklahoma, South Pacific, Porgy and Bess. On Saturday night, Chessie made a float from butter pecan ice cream and milk for a treat. I don't recall whether it was the brand of ice cream or just the times, but sometimes the ice cream still had a tiny piece of the inner shell of a pecan in it, which was jarringly bitter, but the float was still quite the treat. I stayed there a few times myself when I was younger and I still can see the Dippy Bird in her kitchen window perpetually drinking water from a small juice glass, bobbing back and forth, until the water dried up. Then Dippy just looked sad.

If my sister was taken care of and we were old enough to run amok, I mean, take care of ourselves, that meant Pop could go out himself. He had "girlfriends" and romances and, to be fair, often caroused even later than we did. But when my brother and I and Dad each stumbled into the family room Saturday morning at various times of the morning, or early afternoon, I don't remember ever being asked what I did the night before. Perhaps Pop did not want to know. Or perhaps our telling him what we did would necessitate his telling us what he did. And I'm pretty sure I didn't want to know that.

If we had told him what we had done, he would not have been happy. We had held a party, is what the answer would have had to be most summer weekends – a party at his house. In fact, we had parties almost every Friday and Saturday night, especially when the weather was warm and it stayed light until late. Our home on Halifax was party central for about a year. On any given weekend night seventy-five to a hundred kids would pass through the house. Some of them we didn't know. They were acquaintances of friends or even more remote than that. Yes, we really did need more supervision at that point. Kids drank beer and awful cheap apple wine and even one concoction I still recall the recipe for that they called a gin Rickey but it was not like the gin Rickey you would order in a lounge, which is actually a dry cocktail. This one used cheap, oily gin, Wink soda and bottled lime juice. It was made in a gallon jug. If it sounds like we were miscreants, to some extent we were, but remember, there were lots and lots of other teenagers there with us, so we were not alone. A community of scoundrels. We were definitely not alone. Add that to the fact that aiding our bad behavior was pretty much any teenager at that time could drive up to the window of a half dozen liquor stores and buy alcohol without so much as a glance at an I.D. There was one place where you could drive up to the window and order an alcoholic drink to go, served right through the window. Gin and tonic to go, please, served in a plastic cup. They were very different times.

So there we partied, kids getting tipsy, couples fueled by adolescent hormones grappled romantically on couches and in chairs or outside in the yard through any of the sliding glass doors that every room had at least one of. Music blared out of my little phonograph. Zager and Evans warned us of impending doom. Creedence Clearwater foretold a bad moon on the rise. Chicago, Tommy James and the Shondells, Stevie Wonder, Marvin Gaye, The Beatles, The Rolling Stones. It was the heyday of rock. Albums were stacked on the multiple record changer, a new disk plopping atop the previous one when it was finished. We danced. We told bad jokes. Okay, I still tell bad jokes. We laughed and had a great time. No, I don't think Dad wanted to know what we had been doing. Funny thing is, I don't really remember the place being a mess afterwards. Perhaps we at least had enough sense to clean up.

Saturday was Dad's day to grocery shop and run errands. If it was a weekend my sister was at Chessie's, he might bring home beef liver for liver and onions, since he loved it but knew Rhoda couldn't stand it. Or maybe he would start the process of making Wienerschnitzel to have Sunday night. Of course, it all depended on what the A&P had on sale that week. If I was home, I still enjoyed helping put away the groceries, Pop rolling the cans across the black and white tiled floor for me to stack in the cabinets.

More often in those days, however, by Saturday afternoon, I was out running around or working at one of the several part-time jobs I held over those years. I worked for a short time cleaning up a dry cleaners' shop, but the smell of the chemicals both made me feel sick and scared me. I did wonder why the shop did not go up in a puff of biohazardous smoke one day. Then I got a job working at a fast food place called Sir Beef. I can still hear the tune of the commercial advertising the place on television. "Sir Beef, bom, bom, Sir Beef, bom-ba-bom." My job ostensibly was to place the giant beef roasts in the special oven and hit the timer, pressure deep-fry the "Farmer's Daughter Fried Chicken," which was meant to compete with Kentucky Fried Chicken, and, during lunch breaks by other workers, pile the carefully weighed meat on a seeded bun and wrap it in the metallic paper. I liked Sir Beef as a place to get a sandwich. But the new manager, a wormy, gaunt fellow who came in soon after I was hired, took an immediate disliking to me, and tried hard to make my job so miserable that I would quit. I have no idea what I did to deserve the animosity, or why he didn't simply fire me if he wanted me gone, but my first job once he came on was to clean out the walk-in freezer, which honestly desperately needed it. It was very cold work. But having to clean it daily seemed excessive to me. Scraping the various stains off the sidewalk from the sauce packets kids would take outside and stomp on was also pretty distasteful work, but I did it. It was what the manager told me to do.

Late in the summer, Dad was ready to take us on vacation, as he did just about every summer. I asked my father what I should do about my job.

"Ask off." Pop shrugged. "You are not staying here alone." Maybe he did have an inkling what had been going on weekends. I went to work the next afternoon and told the manager about my family's upcoming vacation and asked for the week off.

"No." He glowered at me. "I need people who come to work, not people who take time off." He was wearing a sneer.

"But my father said I couldn't stay here on my own." I couldn't understand his lack of the barest kindness.

"Well, I guess you'll have to quit." He turned to walk away, his job of ruining my day completed.

I shook my head. Jobs for teenagers were pretty abundant in those days. "Okay. I'll be in Wednesday for my check."

"Don't bother." He snarled over his shoulder. I stared at his back as he strutted towards the little office. Wait. He was not only going to make me quit, but he was also going to cheat me out of some twenty bucks? I drove the Corvair home in a funk. I was in disbelief. Really? Just cheat me? I walked into the house and Ernie was there with two of the brutes he kept at his side for protection. These two fellows were behemoths and they were bullies. They actually went out on weekends looking for fights to get into. One stood about six foot two and weighed at least 230 pounds. The other was a bit shorter but he was truly a scary guy who was very powerful and had zero inhibitions when it came to hitting people.

"What's wrong with you?" Ernie saw my glum face. I told them what happened. "What? He said he wouldn't pay you what you are owed?"

"He said, 'Don't bother.'" I held my hands up in defeat.

"Oh, hell no." Ernie stomped out with his minotaurs by his side. "Come on," he called to me from the driveway. We piled into Ernie's muscle car and he peeled his tires as he backed out of the drive. Then he squealed the tires again heading for Frederica Street. I almost felt sorry for what was about to happen to the manager. Almost. We pulled up to the restaurant and Ernie motioned with his hand towards the door. "Let's go get your check."

"Payday isn't until Wednesday."

"Let's go get your check." He opened his door. "You two come with us. We'll make sure he gets paid." I climbed out and followed Ernie in with the enforcers behind me and went inside. The two bullies were ready to pounce. I did start to think that this could actually turn out quite badly.

The manager was in the tiny office, his back to the doorway. Ernie stood aside and motioned for me to step forward. "Excuse me," I said to his back.

"What is it? I thought you quit." He knew my voice.

"But you owe me for nineteen hours of work." I tried to sound intimidating, but the squeak in my voice betrayed my lack of confidence.

"I told you . . ." He turned around to face me and further belittle me, no doubt, when he saw Ernie and the Bouncers (They could become a rock band, perhaps.) behind me wearing menacing grins and punching their ham-sized fists into their hands. I promise you, the two brutes were punching their hands, the message being unmistakable. It was a scene straight from a mobster movie. Ernie was scowling, but the menacing frown was not what got the manager's attention. The blood drained from the manager's face and his jaw dropped. His eyes opened wide. He started shaking visibly and reached into the desk, scratched out a very shaky check for the full amount without even figuring in the withholding. I could see his shirt getting moist. Yes, we meant to scare him into doing what was right, but this poor guy was terrified. "Here." His voice was so shaky, the word had two syllables. I joyfully went outside with the giants behind me. They were yucking it up all the way back to our house how frightened the man had been. I was glad to get paid.

After vacation, I worked briefly as a car hop at the Big Boy Drive-In, which was a little embarrassing, since that meant carrying out an order of fries and a small cola to classmates I would see on Monday. Some of my friends were working as cleaning crews for an operation called Junior Janitorial, and they urged me to get a job there too. Work at night, no weekends, and they had lots of stories about the fun things they did while cleaning the big bank building downtown. I signed on, looking forward to joining the fun. But instead of the bank, I was assigned to a small savings and loan building, which had once been a bank, but I was on my own. No matter, I looked forward to cleaning the place up. It wasn't a very large building, so all I really needed to do was dust, clean the bathrooms, clean the windows, take out the trash, vacuum, mop the marble entrance-way, and polish the 478 foot long brass railing at the entrance. How long could that take? No, the railing was probably only about twelve feet in length, but applying Brasso to it and rubbing it off to a shine took forever, although it did look really nice gleaming in the light. And that meant missing at least part of Rowan and Martin's Laugh-In, and The Mod Squad.

Dad was always proud of us when we showed the initiative to work and tried to encourage our good behavior. One way he did this was to wait dinner until we got home from whatever job we held. Because Dad couldn't start cooking until he got home from work, and many of his dishes were somewhat elaborate in their preparation, we always ate late, even on school nights. I still do. Dinner at seven or seven-thirty was about the norm. And I looked forward to the hot meal. Maybe it was baked chicken leg quarters with rice and a covered glass dish that held pickled beets and onions. Or perhaps it was a ground beef casserole with baked onions on the side. Whatever it was, it would be very welcome after the many long hours toiling in the salt mines for my task masters. Perhaps I overstate the working conditions: they were actually fine.

The best part about being able to drive was we could push our luck in many more and far flung places. We would fill up the trunk on the front of the Corvair with beer and ice and go swimming in cutoffs (or less) in the abandoned strip mines west of town. Once, I was actually persuaded, dared, shamed, pressured into jumping off one of the many cliffs left by the mining process. I struggled up the muddy bank, scratching my arms and legs on the bushes, grasping tiny branches and roots along the way. My head spinning with excitement and too much beer, I stood back, and ran over the edge, throwing myself out to clear the rock formation that jutted out several feet below. As I began my descent, I suddenly realized I had no clue just how deep the water might be or what might be just below the surface made muddy by all the swimmers below. I was suddenly quite sober and terrified. I vowed that if I should live, I would not do that ever again. I kept that vow. But that does not mean I didn't try other equally foolish adventures.

Once we drove up to the sand and gravel company along the river east of town where we decided to swim out to a tree that had been dislodged somewhere upstream and had now wedged itself out in the current some forty yards out in the Mighty Ohio River. It was one of those times when I actually thought: This is how it happens. This is how I could die, swimming against the current of a major river to reach a tree. Another adventure was when my best friend Jimmie and I decided one afternoon to drive down to New Orleans to visit my mother. We had fifty bucks and too much free time. But we made it down there and back safely, if the Corvair did not. It blew out the gaskets and died some seventy miles from home. I do still have fond memories for that sweet little death trap.

We survived adolescence, often more through dumb luck than with good decision-making. We dared, we had adventures, and we learned. Such was the mantra of our times: "Hey fellas, watch this!"

Wienerschnitzel

Serves 6
Ingredients:
2 1/2 pounds veal cutlets (Dad sometimes substituted boneless porkchops)
1/2 cup all-purpose flour
4 tablespoons grated Parmesan cheese
2 eggs
2 teaspoons minced parsley
1/2 teaspoon salt
1/2 teaspoon pepper
1 pinch ground nutmeg
3 tablespoons milk

1 cup dry bread crumbs
6 tablespoons butter
1 large lemon, sliced

Directions:
Place each veal cutlet between two pieces of plastic wrap, and pound with the flat side of a meat mallet until about 1/4 inch thick. Dip in flour to coat.

In a medium bowl, stir together the Parmesan cheese, eggs, parsley, salt, pepper, nutmeg and milk. Place bread crumbs on a plate. Dip each cutlet into the egg mixture, then press in the bread crumbs to coat. Place coated cutlets on a plate and refrigerate for 1 hour or overnight.

Melt butter in a large iron skillet over medium heat. Cook the breaded cutlets until browned on each side, about 3 minutes per side. Remove to a serving platter, and pour the pan juices over them. Garnish with lemon slices.

Dad served egg noodles with this.

Liver and Onions

Serves 4
Ingredients:
2 ½ pounds sliced beef liver
1 1/2 cups milk
1/4 cup butter or margarine, divided
2 large white onions, sliced into rings (I use sweet onions now for this)
2 cups all-purpose flour
salt and pepper to taste

<u>Directions:</u>

Gently rinse liver slices under cold water, and place in a medium bowl. Pour in enough milk to cover. Cover, return to refrigerator and let stand for at least an hour.

Melt 2 tablespoons of butter in a large skillet over medium heat. Separate onion rings, and sauté in butter until soft. Remove onions, and melt remaining butter in the skillet. Season the flour with salt and pepper, and put it in a shallow dish or on a plate. Drain milk from liver, and dredge the liver slices in the flour mixture.

When the butter has melted, turn the heat up to medium-high, and place the coated liver slices in the pan. Cook until nice and brown on the bottom. Turn, and cook on the other side until browned. Add onions and reduce heat to medium. Don't overcook. When the liver is still a little pink in the center when doing a cut test, it is done.

Baked Chicken Leg Quarters

Dad liked to serve this with white rice that he had added a tablespoon and a half of margarine to in the water before cooking. I'm more likely to add a little sesame seed oil to the cooking water, just for flavor.

Serves 4, if you have teenaged sons.

<u>Ingredients:</u>

4 large chicken leg quarters

4 tablespoons butter or margarine, melted

Seasoning salt

Ground black pepper

Paprika

Instructions:

Preheat the oven to 325 degrees.

Arrange the chicken leg quarters in a large baking dish so that they do not touch.

Brush the butter or margarine over each chicken leg quarter. Sprinkle with seasonings.

Cover the pan with foil and bake for 40 minutes.

Increase the oven temperature to 425 degrees, remove the foil and bake for an additional 10-20 minutes until the skin is crisp.

Pickled Beets and Onions

Pop had a glass dish with a glass top he used for this dish. While he generally served dinner, this was one we would pass around and take what we liked.

Ingredients:

2 1/2 cups sliced canned beets, juice reserved

1 large white onion, sliced and divided into rings

1/2 cup apple cider vinegar

2 tablespoons sugar

2 whole cloves

4 black peppercorns

1 bay leaf

3/4 teaspoon salt

Directions:

Place the beets and onions into a glass bowl that has a tight-fitting lid and set aside.

In a medium saucepan, combine vinegar and 1/2 cup of the reserved beet juice and bring to a boil. Add remaining ingredients and return to a boil, stirring to dissolve the sugar. Pour mixture over the beets. Toss until coated, cover and put into refrigerator at least twelve hours. Serve cold.

Cheesy Ground beef Casserole

Serves 6
Ingredients:
1 pound ground beef
1 teaspoon white sugar
1 teaspoon salt
1 teaspoon garlic salt
2 (6 ounce) cans tomato paste
1 ½ cups water
Dash Worcestershire sauce
1 (8 ounce) package egg noodles
1 cup sour cream
1 (3 ounce) package cream cheese, softened
1 large yellow onion, diced
1/2 cup shredded sharp Cheddar cheese, or more to taste

Directions:
Heat a large skillet over medium-high heat. Cook and stir beef in the hot skillet until browned and crumbly, 5 to 7 minutes; drain and discard grease. Mix sugar, salt, garlic salt and tomato paste into ground beef; add water and Worcestershire sauce and simmer until flavors blend, about 20-25 minutes.

Bring a large pot of lightly salted water to a boil. Cook egg noodles in the boiling water, stirring occasionally until cooked through but firm to the bite, about 5 minutes. Drain.

Preheat oven to 350 degrees F. Grease a 9x13-inch casserole dish.

Mix sour cream, cream cheese, and onion in a bowl.

Scoop half the noodles into the prepared casserole dish; top with half the sour cream mixture. Spoon half the ground beef mixture atop sour cream layer. Repeat layering with remaining ingredients. Top casserole with Cheddar cheese.

Bake in the preheated oven until Cheddar cheese has browned, 25 to 30 minutes.

Baked Onions

Serves 4
Ingredients:
4 medium-small white onions, peeled, whole
¼ cup olive oil
½ teaspoon salt
½ teaspoon pepper
½ teaspoon garlic powder

Directions:
Preheat oven to 350 F.

Place onions in a glass baking dish. Pour oil over and turn onions to ensure coverage on all sides of the onions. Season tops with salt, pepper and garlic powder.

Baked to 30 minutes or until onions are cooked through.

Dad's Table

Dad sat at the kitchen table smoking a cigarette. It wasn't dinner time; he just sat there in order to smoke. The ashtray was overflowing with crumpled butts and ashes were sprayed around the table from his haphazard flipping. I sat there with him, talking about his days in the war, his trips into Paris or into small villages to trade rations for cheese, eggs, wine, whatever the people had. Because he had chocolate, he said, he could eat like a king. And there were the misadventures of his compatriots, and the befriending of the little French boy they called Smoky because at the age of eight, he was already begging for cigarettes. The stories were often even told in the same order.

A bead of sweat ran under my shirt. Dad was evidently comfortable, sitting back in his chair, his mind's eye focused on a jeep he and his buddy had "borrowed" to drive to Berlin, although the Americans were still very much in France. Like the other tales, I had heard that one any number of times, but I let him tell it again, in case there was some new detail that might emerge, although there usually wasn't, and just to let him talk. It was as if he had memorized the words of his story sometimes. Other times, it seemed to frustrate him. I wanted to hear the stories, but there was no telling how it might end up. It was a gamble. Several flies had come in through the gaps in the wood-frame screen door, which hung anniegogglin', as Dad said, the hook pretty much keeping the door from falling off completely. The flies took turns buzzing us. Dad pushed up his glasses.

"Harry and I put a new alternator on the jeep outside the officers' club and headed for Berlin. We wanted to have a word or two with Adolph." He chuckled as he shook his head. "That was how they tried to keep people from stealing their jeep, by taking the alternator in with them, but all you had to do was bring your own, so that's what we did. Course, if we'd been caught we would've been in trouble, but it was kind of a musical chairs arrangement anyway. The only reason we had the alternator was because someone had taken our jeep when we had gone into Reims for supplies. Still, it was an officer's jeep, and we were just sergeants, so we would've been in trouble. But only if we got caught." He gave me the same wink he always gave me at that point in the story. I would have been disappointed if he had not done it, I realized. He sat back in the kitchen chair, his arms crossed, the smoke from the Winston in his right hand drifting back from his left shoulder, encasing him like a fog. He paused, looking through the screen door at the mimosa tree in the back yard and I wondered if he had lost his train of thought. The house smelled of stale smoke and apples kept too long in the basket by the sink. The dishes were clean in the drying rack, but cobwebs hung in every corner.

"Is that when you drove across the field and when you got to the other side, you saw the signs in German saying it was a minefield?" I prodded.

"No, no, that was another time when we got a hare-brained idea to go to Paris to find some girls. And we figured after we found some girls, we might just go on over to Nancy, where my father was born, look up some cousins or something and say hello. Hell, Harry didn't care. He'd go anywhere." Dad took another drag on his cigarette. "We had no idea what we were getting into. We knew we wanted out of Camp Lucky Strike, though. That we did know." He blew the smoke out with his words and took another draw and closed his eyes to the sting of the smoke. His arms were thin now, not the sinewy limbs he had used to set up communications over sixty years before, and now they were mottled with liver spots. His hair, once red and wavy, was wispy, white. He retold his stories, as if they needed to be said one last time. "We drove across the field just as happy as we could be, swapping lies about the women we'd been with and all, and then we get to the other side, and here's this big sign in German saying 'Achtung Minen!' We just sat there, not knowing what to do. If we went back, we'd've probably been blown to bits, but we had no idea where we were or how to get home. That was crazy." Dad waved with his cigarette. "Another time, when we were near Compainville, I think it was, I decided to go fishing. I was always looking for something to do and I was sick of the rations and I decided I would go over to the farm next door where they had this big pond and catch some fish. The farmer came out waving at me, yelling, 'Poisson! Poisson!' so I gathered up my tackle and went home. I sure didn't want any poison." Dad grinned. "I had no idea he was telling me it was okay to fish." White stubble was still on his chin. He didn't shave on Sunday. He had on his knit slacks and a short-sleeve button down, also knit, that we had bought him so he wouldn't have to iron any more, since he had nearly burned down the house a few weeks before after leaving the iron on.

"Did you ever get over to Nancy, where our folks are from?" Again, I knew the answer, but wanted to keep him talking. A fly brushed my sweaty temple and I waved it away.

"No, no. Closest I got was Verdun, but by the time I saw it, it was nothing but rubble, hardly a building left standing. Still, the folks were glad to see us, real glad." He leaned forward and flicked the ashes in the general direction of the ashtray, without concern whether he hit his target. He didn't. "Harry and I did go to Paris later, though. After that first time we tried." I had interrupted the pattern and he brought it back. "It was the prettiest place I ever saw. It had just been liberated and folks were all out in the streets, but nobody had any money, so they were eager to, shall we say, trade?" Dad smiled to one side, a wry twist to his face, the same wry twist he used at this point in the story each time. "Girls would come up to us and say, 'Voulez-vous?' and we'd say, 'Let's see what you got,' and they'd yank up their dresses and show us everything." Dad's eyes grew practiced wide. "We'd say, 'Nah,' and walk on down the street." I imagined him, trying to be suave in Paris, this raw young football star from a small Midwestern town who had never even ridden a train before the war broke out.

"So, you never took them up on it?" My tone was purposefully suspicious.

"Well, now, I didn't say that." Dad raised his eyebrows and his thick glasses slipped down his nose and he pushed them back up. He clucked his tongue. "One thing is they told us to stay away from the Bois de Boulogne, said it was dangerous, so, what d'you think Harry and I did?"

"Went to the Bois de Boulogne?" I knew my cue.

"Damn straight. We weren't afraid of a bunch of Frenchies." He made his usual pause. "Scaredest I've been in my whole life." He raised his face to look seriously through his glasses at me. "We went into this little bar and there were the roughest bunch of fellows you ever saw in there, and they would've cut our throats for nothing, just for walking in the place. We went up to the bar, tried to act all brave, but my knees were knocking. We each ordered a beer and stood there back-to-back and drank them down as fast as we could. We sauntered out like we owned the place then ran like hell."

"What happened?"

"We ran down the street and ducked down an alleyway and pretty soon this group of guys from the bar come running past us, so we let them go and ran back up, and ran all the way back up to the arch. I really thought we were done for." A fly landed on the table and I watched it rubbing its legs together. "But we had some good times in Paris, some real good times." Dad let the mysterious tone say what we would not say to me overtly.

"So, you won an all-expenses paid trip to Europe, huh? Courtesy of Uncle Sam." My eye wandered to the dusty shelves. "The way, I see it, you may owe the government some money for all the fringe benefits."

"I paid my share, don't you worry about that." He shooed the fly away from the table. "And you know, it wasn't all fun and games over there. There were these guys called Germans over there who were trying to kill us. Not that you would know anything about that kind of danger." He dismissed me with his hand. I also knew this part, the part where he wasn't real sure I measured up, what with my college education and my refusal to volunteer during the war in Viet Nam. "There were plenty of tough times, kiddo, damned scary times, times when we might've been killed. I remember coming to this one old farmhouse near Soissons and finding the place completely dark, but warm, warm enough for people to be there. It didn't feel right. We had to be careful of the Werewolves, you know. It wasn't a place for the squeamish." He gave me that look that said he meant me. I refused to bite.

"So, what did you do? Blow up the house? Kill everyone in the place?" I knew it would tick him off, but I also hoped that would take him off the tack he had started.

"Blow up the house?" Dad sat back, his eyes widened. "Now, why would I want to do that? If it was okay, it'd be a great place to set up the radio. Glad I didn't, too." He waved at a fly that buzzed in front of him. "Now, I was scared, make no mistake. I was shaking I was so scared." He pulled the cigarettes out of his shirt pocket, shook the pack and gripped the open end so the smokes that jumped up were held there. He placed the pack to his lips and used his mouth to pull out a single cigarette, then lit it with the battered Zippo that lay next to the ashtray. "Harry was with me, of course, and he went around back in case someone ran out the back door. I went up the front steps and kicked in the door. I could hear someone breathing, and I almost started shooting, but then I heard the little boy start crying." Dad shook his head. "I almost shot that boy, and his momma too, for that matter, if I hadn't taken a moment, and that moment was hard, damned hard, because in that moment, I could've been killed." He pointed at me with his cigarette. "And you would never have come into this world." I wasn't sure if he meant that would have been a bad thing or a good thing. "You kids don't have a clue."

"Yeah, I know. We've had it easy." I sat back in my chair. The heat in the room was stifling. The flies circled around the room in a faint buzz.

"Damn straight, you've had it easy. You don't know how easy you've had it." His head was almost hidden by the cloud of cigarette smoke around him.

I stood up now from the table. I had hoped the conversation would not end up here. I walked over to his round-front fridge he had had forever and pulled it open and leaned in to see what was there. "You got anything in here to eat? I'm hungry." The refrigerator was full of margarine tubs and cottage cheese cartons reused for leftovers. I wasn't tempted to open any of them. There was no telling how long they had been in there. He no longer cooked much, but I could still imagine his wonderful spaghetti and meat sauce.

"Ha!" Dad turned in his chair to give me a look. "You haven't been hungry a day in your life!" He pointed at me with his cigarette. "You kids have had everything given to you. You don't know what it means to be hungry. During the depression, we found out what hard times really meant." I straightened and closed the refrigerator and resisted the urge to make up some excuse and simply leave. Dad didn't intend to be mean, I knew; he just sort of fell into it at times. I went back to the table and sat down.

"Can I smoke one of those?" I pointed. Dad raised his eyebrows again. He knew I didn't smoke.

"Sure, kiddo." He handed me the pack and watched me with a bemused smirk on his face. I took one out and lit it up. I had never been much of a smoker and had been told back in school that I didn't look at all natural holding a cigarette, so I tried hard to look like I knew what I was doing. I leaned back in the chair and the smoke drifted into my eyes and I had to blink away the stinging. Dad gave a chuckle. "A little strong for you?" He raised one eyebrow, then shook his head slowly. "Glad you didn't ever start on these." He held up his nearly spent cigarette. "You kids are smarter'n we were." He dragged a last draw and snuffed out the butt. "But you're not braver." I felt a vague headache starting somewhere in the back of my head. A fly landed on the table next to his hand. He kept his eyes glued on me, then snatched the fly off the table with a flick of his hand. He stood up quickly, marched over to the sink, and slammed the fly down the drain, running water to complete the flush. He washed his hands, then came over to the table and sat down, rather smugly I thought. "And I'm not dead yet."

He looked at the barely smoked cigarette I had crushed into the ashtray when he had gotten up and frowned. "They're not free, you know."

"Yeah, I know. I'll buy you a pack when we go out for lunch."

"You want to go out? I've got plenty of food here. No need to spend all that money when I've got lots of stuff here." I considered a lunch of Spam and creamed corn in a hot kitchen filled with cigarette smoke and flies and decided against it.

"No, I'd like to take you out for lunch, Dad. Where do you want to go?"

"I hate for you to spend money when we've got food."

"I insist." I leaned up in the chair. A fly buzzed past my head and I snatched it out of the air without looking. The fly buzzed in my hand. Dad's eyes widened and he watched me as I marched over to the sink and slammed the fly down, flushed it, and washed my hands in impersonation of his movements. It was a lucky grab, but I wasn't about to let it pass.

Dad gave me a grin. "I like Ponderosa," he offered.

"Works for me." I reached into my pocket for my keys.

Dad stood, shook his head, and gave me a strong pat on the back as we headed for the door.

Pop's Spaghetti Sauce

Feeds: small army
Ingredients:
1 pound ground chuck
2 teaspoons olive oil
3 garlic cloves, minced
1 medium Vidalia or white onion, diced
1 bell pepper, diced

7-8 mushrooms, sliced

2 6 oz. cans tomato paste

2 cups water

1 tablespoon red wine (not too much)

Several good dashes Worcestershire sauce

1 tablespoon each dried oregano and basil

1 teaspoon dry mustard

½ teaspoon paprika

Dash cayenne

1 teaspoon sugar

Salt and pepper

Half a can of black olives, sliced (optional)

4-6 oz. sliced pepperoni (optional)

Directions:

In a large Dutch oven or heavy pan, crumble and brown the chuck over medium low heat, then drain using a metal colander placed over a trash can. While draining the meat, add oil to the pan and add next 4 ingredients. Cook over medium low until vegetables are soft but not brown. Add next 10 ingredients and the drained chuck and season to taste. Cook over very low heat for at least 45 minutes for flavors to marry. Add olives and pepperoni for last 10 minutes, if desired. Serve over al dente pasta. Any leftovers freeze well in a Ziplock if you squeeze out the air.

The Recipes

1. Hasenpfeffer
2. Chicken cacciatore
3. Clabber milk
4. Soda bread
5. Ham steak
6. Cheese grits
7. Little meat sauce diablo
8. Veal roast with lardons and potatoes
9. Eggs with a hat
10. Welsh rarebit
11. Beef roast with ginger snaps
12. Stewed Beef heart
13. Baked chicken with herbs
14. Canned fruit salad
15. Beef stroganoff
16. Broiled steak with pepper, onions and mushrooms
17. Mushrooms on English muffins
18. Tomato aspic
19. Braised spare ribs
20. Boston brown bread
21. Sauerbraten
22. Meat loaf
23. Stewed tomatoes
24. Lasagna

25. Shrimp with cocktail and remoulade sauces
26. Eggs salad dinner
27. Grilled steak with peppers and onions
28. Dad's grilled hamburgers
29. Potato salad
30. Three-bean salad
31. German potato salad
32. Corn pudding
33. Stuffed pork chops
34. Glazed ham
35. Peccadillo
36. Brains and eggs
37. Beef tongue
38. Octopus pizza
39. Pork chops Provençale
40. Cottage fries
41. Stuffed peppers
42. Pineapple Upside Down Cake
43. Duck a l'orange
44. Leg of lamb with mint jelly
45. Scalloped oysters
46. Roast turkey
47. Giblet gravy
48. Turkey hash
49. Turkey a la king
50. Turkey tetrazzini
51. Turkey and rice soup
52. Creamed onions
53. Sweet potato casserole
54. Stuffed pork roast with port reduction
55. Apple walnut dressing
56. Devilled eggs

57. Au gratin potatoes
58. Beef and kidney pie
59. Baked apples
60. Salt herring
61. Corned beef brisket
62. Boston baked beans
63. Liver and onions
64. Weinerschnitzel
65. Baked chicken leg quarters
66. Pickled beets and onions
67. Cheesy ground beef casserole
68. Baked onions
69. Spaghetti sauce

About the Author

Lawrence Weill is an author and artist in far western Kentucky. His previous books include *Out in Front, Incarnate, I'm in the Room*, and *The Path of Rainwater*. His short fiction, poetry and nonfiction have appeared in a wide range of local, regional, and national journals. He also is a visual artist working in graphite, watercolors, oils, metal, glass and wood. Lawrence lives in the woods overlooking a beaver pond next to a wildlife preserve.

Made in the USA
Middletown, DE
15 September 2022

10495806R00151